SCOTTISH MISCELLANY

EVERYTHING YOU ALWAYS WANTED TO KNOW ABOUT SCOTLAND THE BRAVE

By
JONATHAN GREEN

Skyhorse Publishing

Skyhorse Publishing books may be purchased in bulk at special discounts for sales promotion, corporate gifts, fund-raising, or educational purposes. Special editions can also be created to specifications. For details, contact the Special Sales Department, Skyhorse Publishing, 307 West 36th Street, 11th Floor, New York, NY 10018 or info@skyhorsepublishing.com.

Skyhorse® and Skyhorse Publishing® are registered trademarks of Skyhorse Publishing, Inc.®, a Delaware corporation.

Visit our website at www.skyhorsepublishing.com.

10 9 8 7 6 5

Library of Congress Cataloging-in-Publication Data is available on file.

ISBN: 978-1-62873-719-6

Printed in China

FOR

WENDY

CONTENTS

INTRODUCTION

"The English are not happy unless they are miserable, the Irish are not at peace unless they are at war, and the Scots are not at home unless they are abroad."

—George Orwell

What do you think of when you think of Scotland? Men in skirts—sorry—kilts? Bagpipes? Haggis? Whisky? Shortbread? The Edinburgh Fringe? The Duke of Edinburgh perhaps? The Loch Ness Monster? Tartan? Mel Gibson with half his face painted blue shouting "Freedom!"? Christopher Lambert declaring that he is "Connor MacLeod of the Clan MacLeod!" in stilted English with a Gallic accent?

Whatever it is that you most associate with Scotland, have you ever wondered why all these things have become so associated with the Land of the Brave? Why do the Scots wear tartan, for instance? Why do they celebrate Burns' Night? Why is the thistle the Scottish national flower? Who decided that something that sounds like a cat being strangled would make a pleasant musical instrument anyway? Do Scotsmen really say "Och aye the noo," and, if so, what does it actually mean? And why is Scotland called Scotland, for that matter?

Of course, the history of the United States and Scotland are inextricably linked as well. From the 1760s until well into Queen Victoria's reign, landowners systematically turned people off the land they had farmed for hundreds of years to make room for them to graze herds of sheep and cattle, as part of a process now known as the "Highland Clearances." Many of the people evicted in this way emigrated to North America. Some found work on farms and plantations in Canada and the United States, and there they stayed.

Nine governors of the original thirteen American states were Scots. Senate Resolution 155, passed on 20 March 1998, referred to the predominance of Scots among the Founding Fathers and claimed that the American Declaration of Independence was modeled on the Declaration of Arbroath, an eloquent appeal for the recognition of Scottish independence and sovereignty, signed on 6 April 1320. A Scotsman, one John Paul Jones, formed the United States Navy; the entire crew of the *Enola Gay*, the plane that dropped the American atomic bomb on Hiroshima, Japan, during World War II, were of Scots descent; and one of the richest men in the world, Bill Gates, cofounder of Microsoft, is of Scottish American descent. Indeed, there are an estimated six million Americans of Scottish descent living in the United States today.

You will discover many more facts like these throughout this book. Whether you are Scottish or of Scottish descent, or if you are just interested in Scotland and its people, its history, its heritage, its culture and its curiosities, there's something for everyone in this book.

Where to begin?

Before we set about uncovering the origins of the nation, its people, and some of its more curious pastimes, perhaps we should first solve the puzzle as to why Scotland is called Scotland at all. And what that fact has to do with an Egyptian princess . . .

WHAT DOES AN EGYPTIAN
PRINCESS HAVE TO DO WITH
THE BIRTH OF SCOTLAND?

I t may surprise you to learn that the country we know today as Scotland has only been in existence for roughly 1,100 years. Before that it was known as Pictland and, before that, Alba or Caledonia. It wasn't until the late 800s that references to Pictland in the ancient chronicles are superseded by references to Scotland. Where did the name "Scotland" come from in the first place?

Scotland is named after a Gaelic tribe who originally came from Ireland. They knew themselves as the Gaels, and they settled in what we now know as Scotland from the fifth or sixth century onward, migrating first into the Scottish islands and from there to the mainland. By the eleventh century they had come to dominate the whole of mainland Scotland.

However, these Gaels traced their roots back hundreds, if not thousands, of years into the mists of the time before recorded history and myth, to the mother of their race, Scota. After all, as Eurmeus wrote in 316 BC, myths were really history in disguise. As with so many myths, there are variations on that of Scota.

Scota is the name given to two different mythological daughters of two different Egyptian pharaohs. It was actually from these pharaohs that the Gaels traced the origin of their people. According to one account, Scota was the wife of Mil and the daughter of a pharaoh called Nectanebus. In this version of the myth, the sons of Mil and Scota settled in Ireland before invading what was to become Scotland.

However, according to the version of the story recorded in the early Irish chronicle *Lebor Gabála Érenn,* Scota was the daughter of a pharaoh called Cingris, a name

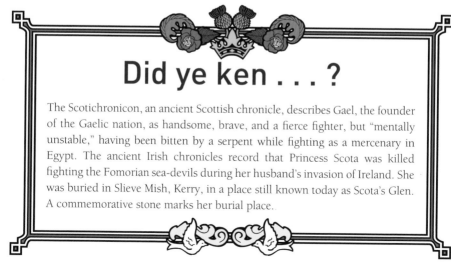

Did ye ken . . . ?

The Scotichronicon, an ancient Scottish chronicle, describes Gael, the founder of the Gaelic nation, as handsome, brave, and a fierce fighter, but "mentally unstable," having been bitten by a serpent while fighting as a mercenary in Egypt. The ancient Irish chronicles record that Princess Scota was killed fighting the Fomorian sea-devils during her husband's invasion of Ireland. She was buried in Slieve Mish, Kerry, in a place still known today as Scota's Glen. A commemorative stone marks her burial place.

What does an Egyptian princess have to do with the birth of Scotland? | 3

Did ye ken . . . ?

The part of the mainland where the Gaels first settled became known as Airer Gaedel, meaning "the coast of the Gaels," which is now more commonly known as Argyll, where the sweaters come from.

that is only found in Irish legend. This Scota married Niul, the son of Fenius Faraid, a Babylonian who traveled to Scythia after the destruction of the Tower of Babel, as recorded in the Book of Genesis. Appropriately enough for someone associated with the Tower of Babel, Niul was a scholar of languages and, in this capacity, was invited by Cingris to Egypt, where he was promptly offered Scota's hand in marriage. The son born of their union was Goídel Glas, the ancestor of the Gaels. He was also the creator of the Gaelic language, a feat he supposedly managed by combining the best features of all of the seventy-two languages in existence at the time.

From here on in, the facts (if we can call them that) get a little hazy. Either Goídel or his son Sru was expelled from Egypt shortly after the Exodus of the Israelites by yet another pharaoh that one Irish chronicler calls Intuir. After much traveling throughout the ancient world, his descendants settled in the Iberian peninsula (in what is modern Spain and Portugal). It was here that Mil Espáine was born. His sons—Eber Finn and Eremon—established a Gaelic presence in Ireland.

To demonstrate just how confusing alternate versions of the same myth can be, in *The Story of the Irish Race,* by Seumas MacManus, Scota married Niul, who was the grandson of Gaodhal Glas. Then a completely different Scota altogether—who was coincidentally the daughter of another pharaoh—married Miled (or Milesius, as he is also known). According to MacManus, it was this second Scota who left Iberia

with her eight sons and their families, after Miled died, eventually settling in Ireland. According to this version of events, a number of Scota's sons died during the sea voyage to Ireland due to a terrible storm. Queen Scota herself, however, made it to Ireland, only to die during the battle that took place between the Milesians and the Tuatha Dé Danann—the tribes of the Earth Goddess who were already living in Ireland. In yet another version of the story, Scota and Goídel Glas were wife and husband, rather than mother and son. Confusing, isn't it?

Whatever the truth of Scota and her family's long journey from Egypt to Ireland, and from there to Scotland, what is known is that the name Scotland comes from the Latin *Scoti*, which was the name given to the Gaels from Ireland by the Romans, and was their word for pirates or raiders. *Scotia* was the name initially used by the Romans to refer to Ireland, not Scotland, but by the eleventh century *Scotia* was also being used to refer to the Gaelic-dominated part of the country north of the River Forth.

These Gaels were full of energy and creative spirit, and it was they who ultimately joined together the different races of the north into one kingdom. It wasn't until the late Middle Ages that the words *Scots* (for the people) and *Scotland* (for the country) were used to describe what we now think of as the Land of the Free. At the time of the English king Edward I—known as the Hammer of the Scots—the Scots themselves made much of their link with the Egyptian princess Scota, even going so far as to claim that they were descended from Noah the Ark-builder.

Of course modern Scotland is part of the nation of Great Britain, which, along with Northern Ireland and various island groups such as the Isles of Scilly, the Hebrides, Shetland Islands, and Orkney Islands, make up the United Kingdom. Of the 88,795 square miles (229,979 square kilometers) of land that make up Great Britain, 30,414 square miles (78,772 square kilometers) is Scotland.

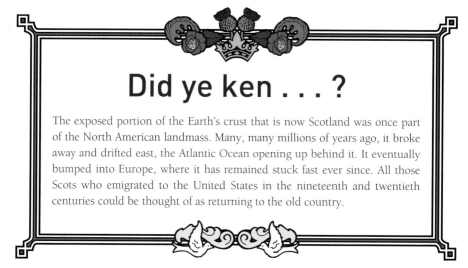

Did ye ken . . . ?

The exposed portion of the Earth's crust that is now Scotland was once part of the North American landmass. Many, many millions of years ago, it broke away and drifted east, the Atlantic Ocean opening up behind it. It eventually bumped into Europe, where it has remained stuck fast ever since. All those Scots who emigrated to the United States in the nineteenth and twentieth centuries could be thought of as returning to the old country.

WHAT IS THE SCOTTISH NATIONAL ANTHEM?

This is something of a trick question, since Scotland is one of the constituent countries of the United Kingdom. As such, its national anthem is "God Save the Queen," just as it is for England, Wales, and Northern Ireland. Scotland has no distinct official national anthem of its own. (Note the word "official" in that last sentence.)

Britain was the first country in the world to have a national anthem. In its present form it dates from 1745, which is, coincidentally, the same year that Bonnie Prince Charlie attempted to wrest the Scottish throne from England again during the Jacobite Rebellion. Britain is a democratic monarchy. The head of state is Queen Elizabeth II, and she is also head of the Commonwealth, which unites fifty-four countries that used to be governed by Britain. However, despite having the same basic unit of currency, the pound sterling (£), with one pound being divided into 100 pennies, Scotland has different banknotes from the rest of Britain, and still has a £1 note, whereas in the rest of Britain the £1 note was replaced by a coin (first issued in 1983).

As well as having their own variation on a common currency, some Scots would also like Scotland to have its own unique national anthem. And there are certainly a number of contenders for the title of unofficial national anthem of Scotland.

The first and most high profile of these is "Flower of Scotland." It is played at events such as football (soccer) and rugby matches that involve the Scottish national team. It was written in 1967 by Roy Williamson of popular Scottish folk group the Corries and refers to the victory of the Scots over the English at the Battle of Bannockburn. (We'll come back to Bannockburn later.) The words are as follows:

O Flower of Scotland,
When will we see
Your like again
That fought and died for
Your wee bit Hill and Glen
And stood against him
Proud Edward's army
And sent him homeward.
Tae think again.
The Hills are bare now,
And Autumn leaves
Lie thick and still,
O'er land that is lost now,
Which those so dearly held,
That stood against him,
Proud Edward's Army,
And sent him homeward,
Tae think again.

Those days are past now,
And in the past
They must remain,
But we can still rise now,
And be the nation again,
That stood against him,
Proud Edward's Army,
And sent him homeward,
Tae think again.

The "Flower of Scotland" mentioned in the song is actually Robert the Bruce. This allegedly spider-inspired, cave-dwelling Scottish monarch had rebelled against the English and laid siege to Stirling Castle as part of his struggle for Scottish independence. Edward II retaliated; however, the Bruce's army trounced Edward II's English forces on Scottish soil on 23–24 June 1314.

The song was first used by the national rugby union team of Scotland in 1974, when the winger Billy Steele encouraged his teammates to sing it on the Lions' victor tour of South Africa. The song was adopted as the pregame anthem during the 1990 Five Nations Championship, which happened to culminate in a deciding match between Scotland and England. Scotland won the match 13–7, which meant they won the Grand Slam. The Scottish Football Association officially adopted "Flower of Scotland" as its pregame anthem in 1997, although it had been used by them before then.

Did ye ken . . . ?

The tune to which "Flower of Scotland" is sung was originally composed on the Northumbrian smallpipes, which are different than the traditional bagpipes in that they play in F and have the benefit of keys on the chanter to achieve a greater range of notes.

Another suitable anthem could be "Scotland the Brave." This song is already used for the Scottish team at the Commonwealth Games, until it was replaced by—you've guessed it!—"Flower of Scotland" in time for the 2010 games held in Delhi.

Hark! When the night is falling,
Hark! Hear the pipes are calling,
Loudly and proudly calling, down through the glen.
There where the hills are sleeping,

Now feel the blood a-leaping,
High as the spirits of the old Highland men.

> *Chorus*
> *Towering in gallant fame,*
> *Scotland my mountain hame,*
> *High may your proud standards gloriously wave,*
> *Land of my high endeavour,*
> *Land of the shining river,*
> *Land of my heart for ever, Scotland the brave.*

High in the misty Highlands,
Out by the purple islands,
Brave are the hearts that beat beneath Scottish skies.
Wild are the winds to meet you,
Staunch are the friends that greet you,
Kind as the love that shines from fair maidens' eyes.

> *Chorus*
> *Towering in gallant fame . . .*

Far off in sunlit places,
Sad are the Scottish faces,
Yearning to feel the kiss of sweet Scottish rain.
Where tropic skies are beaming,
Love sets the heart a-dreaming,
Longing and dreaming for the homeland again.

> *Chorus*
> *Towering in gallant fame . . .*

Did ye ken . . . ?

"Highland Cathedral" is a popular Scottish bagpipe melody, even though it was actually written by two German musicians, Ulrich Roever and Michael Korb, for the 1982 Highland Games. It has subsequently undergone various orchestrations and had lyrics added in English and in Scottish Gaelic. The tune was also the anthem of the Royal Hong Kong Police when Hong Kong was still under British rule. It was played at a ceremonial lowering of the governor's flag at Chris Patten's residence, Government House, on the last day of British rule in 1997.

Did ye ken . . . ?

"Scots Wha Hae" is the party song of the Scottish National Party and is sung at the close of their annual national conference each year.

"Scotland the Brave" is another relatively recent creation. The tune probably first appeared around the turn of the twentieth century, and at that time was already known as "Scotland the Brave." However, the lyrics to go with it weren't written until 1950, by one Cliff Hanley, a Scottish journalist, for the well-known singer Robert Wilson to perform.

The tune also happens to be the authorized pipe band march of the British Columbia Dragoons of the Canadian Forces. As a consequence, it is played during the Pass in Review at Friday parades at The Citadel. In 2006, it was also adopted as the regimental quick march of the Royal Regiment of Scotland. Long before that, during the 1982 and 1986 World Cup competitions, the Scottish national team used "Scotland the Brave" as its anthem.

Since devolution of power to the re-formed Scottish Parliament, there has been more serious discussion of a national anthem for Scotland. This has, in turn, led to the suitability of "Flower of Scotland" being disputed. Other suggestions have included "Highland Cathedral," "Scots Wha Hae," and "A Man's a Man for a' That."

"Is There for Honest Poverty," which is better known as "A Man's a Man for a' That," is a Scots song by Robert Burns. It was sung by renowned Scottish folksinger Sheena Wellington at the opening of the Scottish Parliament in May 1999. It was also sung at the funeral of Donald Dewar, the inaugural First Minister of Scotland, in 2000.

"Scots Wha Hae" (meaning "Scots, Who Have") is another patriotic Scottish song by Robert Burns, and until it was supplanted by "Scotland the Brave" and "Flower of Scotland," it served for a long time as the unofficial national anthem of the country. Written in 1793, it takes the form of a speech given by Robert the Bruce before the Battle of Bannockburn in 1314, the outcome of which meant that Scotland maintained its sovereignty. Burns wrote the lyrics to fit the traditional Scottish tune "Hey Tuttie Tatie," which, according to tradition, was supposed to have been played by Bruce's army at the battle itself, initially giving it the title "Robert Bruce's March to Bannockburn."

Burns claimed that he had been inspired by Bruce's "glorious struggle for Freedom, associated with the glowing ideas of some other struggles of the same nature, not quite so ancient." The song was included in the 1799 edition of *A Select*

Collection of Original Scottish Airs for the Voice, edited by George Thomson, who preferred the tune "Lewie Gordon" and, as a result, had Burns add to the fourth line of each stanza to make it fit. However, in the 1802 edition, the original words and choice of tune were restored.

In July 2006, the Royal Scottish National Orchestra conducted an online poll asking people to choose a national anthem for Scotland from the five tunes mentioned above. Ten thousand people dutifully took part and voted. It was "Flower of Scotland" that came out on top in the end, with 41 percent of the vote. The official national anthem is still "God Save the Queen," at least for the time being.

WHO BUILT HADRIAN'S WALL AND WHY?

It may be named after the Roman emperor Hadrian (AD 76–138), during whose reign it was built, but Hadrian didn't so much as lay a foundation stone himself, although he did visit Britain and the ultimate limit of his empire, better known to us today as Scotland.

Britain lay at the corner of the enormous Roman Empire, more than 1,200 kilometers from Rome itself. A treacherous sea cut it off from mainland Europe. Many British tribes, such as the Caledonii and Brigantes of the north, threatened rebellion. The Romans controlled this remote province with their army—Roman soldiers were the strongest, best-trained, and best-armed soldiers in the world. The Roman army arrived in the region we now know as Scotland around AD 80. They built forts and roads over the Lowlands and marched into the Highlands. They called the people who lived there *Picti*, meaning "painted ones."

Unlike England, Scotland was never part of the Roman Empire, despite repeated attempts to subdue the Highlands and bring them under Roman rule. It was the island's precious tin reserves that brought the Romans to Britain in the first place. Once there they set about indoctrinating the native peoples in the ways of Roman civilization—meaning straight roads, indoor plumbing, central heating, and toga parties. The Picts proved resistant to the lures of Roman life.

A number of Roman incursions were mounted from the north of England, the first being led by Gnaeus Julius Agricola in AD 79–80, on behalf of the then Emperor Vespasian. Setting out from Carlisle he reached the Forth-Clyde isthmus, where he set up a line of defenses, with scouting parties penetrating as far as Perthshire. In AD 82 he came north again, focusing on what is now Galloway and Ayrshire, in an attempt to conquer the Novante tribe. In AD 83 he made it as far as Angus and Aberdeenshire. Agricola's conquests were eventually consolidated with another advance up the east coast, which culminated with victory over the Caledonii tribe at Mons Graupius.

The only record we have of this important event is that of the Roman historian Tacitus. The first Scot—or perhaps more accurately the first Pict, or even Caledonian—named in history is Calgacus the Swordsman. He addresses the Romans before the battle with this rousing speech: "We, the choicest flower of Britain's manhood, were hidden away in her most secret places. Out of sight we were kept from the defilement of tyranny. We, the most distant dwellers upon Earth, the last of the free."

However, it is perfectly likely that Calgacus didn't actually exist and that he was in fact an invention of Tacitus himself, who wrote about his defeat at the hands of the Romans twenty years

Did ye ken . . . ?

Many people believe that the people already living in Britain when the Romans invaded were the Celts. However, the Celts didn't actually arrive in England until long after the Romans had left; they actually arrived on 21 June 1792. It was on this date that a group of London "bards" enacted an entirely invented ceremony on Primrose Hill in London, claiming they were reviving a ritual established by the Celtic nation and its druids. However, before this there is no record of the pre-Roman inhabitants of Britain being referred to as Celts. The word "Celt" actually comes from the Greek historian Herodotus, writing in 450 BC, to refer to the peoples who lived around the headwaters of the Danube north of the Alps. Most historians now believe that the language and culture we call "Celtic" today spread by contact rather than invasion, with groups of people becoming "Celtic" (for want of a better word) by adopting the architecture, fashions, and ways of speaking that were useful or attractive to them, and not due to sharing an ethnic background.

after the Battle of Mons Graupius had taken place; a reminder that history is written by the winners.

In AD 87, Agricola returned to Rome and all that he had achieved in Scotland was soon to be overturned. Although the Romans had beaten the Picts in battle, they remained unable to conquer Pictland (as the area was then called), so they decided to wall it off altogether. The Romans had officially retreated, and in AD 118 the Emperor Hadrian commanded that his famous wall be built from the Solway Firth to the North Sea to separate the rebellious Brigantes from the unruly northern tribes. According to the emperor's biographer, Hadrian was, "the first to build a wall, eighty miles long, to separate the Romans from the barbarians."

The army headquarters were at Carlisle. Soldiers patrolled the wall night and day, watching both sides for enemy movements. Summer might be warm, but woollen cloaks and leggings were needed for the cold, wet winters. A posting to this edge of the empire fortification was seen as the short straw in terms of military tours of duty.

The accepted view is that Hadrian's Wall was constructed to keep the Scots out, although a Scotsman might say it was built to stop the English escaping to the Scots' beautiful country. Whatever the truth of the matter, construction of the wall was begun in AD 122 and took between six and eight years to complete. When finished it measured 74 miles (199 kilometers) in length (which is the same as 80 Roman miles) and was 15 feet (5 meters) high in places and 10 feet (3 meters) deep. There were fortified milecastles (or gateways) every mile, with two lookout towers between each one. The actual building work was carried out by members of the second, sixth, and twentieth legions (providing a workforce of 5,000–15,000) with each century (a unit of eighty men) being allocated a length of wall to build. The project manager on the job was the governor of Britain at the time, Aulus Platorius Nepos. The last fort, Carrawburgh, was completed between AD 130 and 133 and it is quite likely that work on the wall was still happening when Hadrian died in AD 138. Settlements soon grew up around the forts and trading centers were created. For three hundred years Hadrian's Wall stood as the Roman Empire's most imposing frontier.

The ruins of Hadrian's Wall still stand today, a testament to the civil engineering skills of the Romans but also to the recalcitrant nature of the Scots (or rather the Picts, at the time), who would not be dominated by anyone, although it is actually south of what is now Scotland's border with England. Surprisingly, perhaps, the only ancient source for its provenance is the Augustan History and no sources survive to confirm what the wall was called in antiquity; neither is there an historical literary source that gives its name.

In AD 138–139 Emperor Antoninus Pius again ordered the governor of Britannia to subdue the Lowland tribes. The structure that now bears his name, the Antonine Wall, was turf-built and fronted by a defensive ditch that was wider and deeper than that before Hadrian's Wall. It stands between Bridgeness on the Forth and Old Kilpatrick on the Clyde.

The last attempt by the Romans to invade Scotland was undertaken in AD 306 by Emperor Constantius and his son Constantine, and there are also reports of punitive advances led by Constantine's son Julian. By this time the Picti were on the offensive themselves and come AD 367, Picts and Scots had overrun Hadrian's

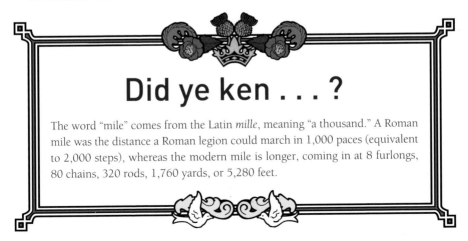

Did ye ken . . . ?

The word "mile" comes from the Latin *mille*, meaning "a thousand." A Roman mile was the distance a Roman legion could march in 1,000 paces (equivalent to 2,000 steps), whereas the modern mile is longer, coming in at 8 furlongs, 80 chains, 320 rods, 1,760 yards, or 5,280 feet.

Wall, the Romans' last great defensive line, and by AD 400 it had been abandoned. Stones taken from the ruins of Hadrian's Wall were used to build local buildings and for the construction of great monastery complexes such as those at Lindisfarne and Jarrow Priory.

Roman troops began to withdraw from Britain to defend their homeland from increasingly ferocious attacks by the Visigoths and Huns of Germany, and after they left Britain altogether in about AD 407, power fell into the hands of other invaders. From Ireland came the Scots, who established colonies on what is now the west coast of Scotland. From the far north came the Picts. The strongest and most successful groups came from northwest Europe, mainly Denmark and northern Germany. These were the Angles, Saxons, and Jutes—now known as the Anglo-Saxons. The age of the English had arrived.

Did ye ken . . . ?

Much of Hadrian's Wall has now disappeared. The preservation of what remains can be credited to one man, John Clayton, a lawyer who became town clerk of Newcastle in the 1830s. Enthusiastic about preserving the wall, in order to prevent farmers taking stones from the wall, he began buying some of the land on which it stood. He carried out excavation work at a fort at Cilurnum, as well as at the better-known Housesteads, and even excavated some of the milecastles. By managing the farms he had acquired, Clayton succeeded in improving both the land and the livestock, which in turn produced cash that could be invested in future restoration work.

Hadrian's Wall was declared a UNESCO World Heritage Site in 1987, becoming part of the larger "Frontiers of the Roman Empire" World Heritage Site in 2005. In 2003, a National Trail footpath was opened which follows the line of the wall from Wallsend to Bowness-on-Solway, but because of the fragile nature of the landscape in which it stands, walkers are asked to follow the path only during the summer months.

WHY IS ANDREW THE PATRON SAINT OF SCOTLAND?

Y ou may be surprised to learn that when it comes to the day dedicated to Scotland's own patron saint, more of a fuss is made of it by Scots living abroad than by those living in Scotland itself. It isn't even a public holiday in Scotland. As is so often the way, expat Scots are demonstrably more patriotic than those living within the Highlands and Lowlands of Caledonia itself.

Although Andrew is now regarded as a good Scottish name, it originated, along with the patron saint, in the Holy Land. Saint Andrew (who died circa AD 60) started out in life as a fisherman. His home was at Capernaum, a settlement on the shore of the Sea of Galilee, and he was the brother of Simon Peter.

Andrew was actually a disciple of John the Baptist before he became a follower of Christ. In all four of the Gospels he is listed as being among the first four of Jesus' apostles. He gets a special mention in the Bible for the part he played in the feeding of the five thousand (Matthew 14:15–21) and also in the matter of the Greeks who wished to meet with Jesus (John 12:20–2).

Despite being such an important figure in the New Testament, scholars are not sure where he preached the Gospel (both Scythia and Epirus in Greece claimed him as their apostle), where he died, or even where he was buried. However, the manner of his death is very well-documented.

According to tradition, Patras in Achaia (in modern-day Greece) is said to be the place where Andrew was put to death as a martyr. He was reputedly crucified on an X-shaped cross, preaching to the people there for two days before he finally succumbed and died.

Beginning in the sixth century, his feast day of 30 November was universally recognized and celebrated. Churches were dedicated to him from early times in Italy, France, and Anglo-Saxon England, where the earliest was in Rochester, in the county of Kent, the Garden of England.

As is the case for most saints, a number of legends that have grown up about the life and holy work of St Andrew. One of these, regarding a journey to Ethiopia, is told in the Old English poem "Andreas." But none of this explains how he came to be the patron saint of Scotland.

He was actually adopted as patron by a Pictish king Angus, who was supposed to have seen a vision—an image of the cross appeared in the heavens during a decisive battle. The saint's relics were brought from Patras all the way to Fife by St Regulus, where he stopped at the place that now bears the saint's name, the Cathedral of St Andrew.

Having no obvious industrial and commercial assets, St Andrews nonetheless became the ecclesiastical capital of Scotland, a place of great political importance, and its first seat of scholarship. The University of St Andrews was founded in 1413, making it the oldest university in Scotland and the third oldest in the English-speaking world. Its motto, *Aien Aristeuein,* means "Always strive to be the best." The city's other "royal and ancient" institution is, naturally, that of golf!

The office of rector at the University of St Andrews is derived from an Act of 1858, which created the position as the president of the University Court. This rectorship is of particular interest, because it is elected by the university's student body, which may explain the roll call of rectors since 1970:

John Cleese	1970	Nicholas Campbell	1991
Alan Coren	1973	Donald Findlay QC	1993
Frank Muir	1976	Andrew Neil	1999
Tim Brooke-Taylor	1979	Sir Clement Freud	2002
Katharine Whitehorn	1982	Simon Pepper	2005
Stanley Adams	1985	Kevin Dunion	2008
Nicholas Parsons	1988		

The university awards the annual Frank Muir Prize for Humour, currently worth £400, to the student who submits the most humorous and witty original composition addressing an aspect of life at St Andrews.

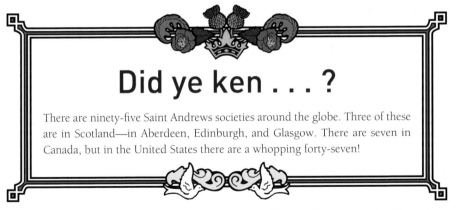

Did ye ken . . . ?

There are ninety-five Saint Andrews societies around the globe. Three of these are in Scotland—in Aberdeen, Edinburgh, and Glasgow. There are seven in Canada, but in the United States there are a whopping forty-seven!

Interestingly, it is Saint Ninian who is known as Scotland's *own* apostle. Ninian is the first missionary into Scotland of whom we have any certain knowledge. Accepted wisdom used to have it that Ninian was a native of Cumbria who was sent by Rome to convert the Picts in the fourth and fifth centuries AD. He was supposed to have been the son of a converted British chieftain and certainly it is likely that there were Christians in Roman Scotland, whether serving in the legions or trading with the forts and the tribesmen, or even shivering up on top of Hadrian's Wall on the lookout for invading Picts.

Ninian founded a church at Whithorn in Galloway, where he was bishop, and he is the first named Christian of Scottish record, appearing, as he does, in Bede's *Historica Ecclesiastica.* His association with the foundation at Whithorn, however, remains a matter of legend rather than of fact. No fifth-century archaeological remains have been found at Whithorn, which some spoilsports say may originally have been a sixth-century Irish monastic settlement anyway.

However, scholars now believe that there may have been two Ninians; or indeed that a scribe of the old Church mixed him up with one of Columba's mentors, and that he is really just a spelling mistake! It has also been suggested that Ninian's life may be a fabrication, designed to bolster some clerical faction or other.

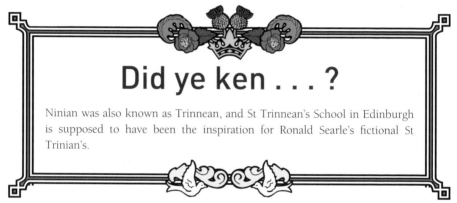

Did ye ken . . . ?

Ninian was also known as Trinnean, and St Trinnean's School in Edinburgh is supposed to have been the inspiration for Ronald Searle's fictional St Trinian's.

Whether he truly existed or not, the next saint of note who made a big impression on what we now know as Scotland was Saint Columba (c. 521–97). Both his Latinized name, Columba, and its Gaelic equivalent, *Columcille,* mean "dove," but rather than being born a peacemaker, he actually came from a warring royal lineage. Battles over monastic possessions in Ireland led to his banishment from Ulster and exile to the island of Iona in 563, with twelve of his closest companions.

Did ye ken . . . ?

It could be argued that Columba started the first copyright war in publishing history after he illegally copied one of Abbot Finnia of Clonard's prized psalters. This theft of what we now call "intellectual property rights" led directly to the Battle of Cooldrevny in AD 561, in which as many as three thousand warriors may have died, and it was this battle over monastic possessions that saw him exiled to Iona.

It was on Iona that he founded the now world-famous monastery from which he carried out his missionary work with zeal. The island provided a strong strategic base for these early missionaries, halfway between the territory of the Scots of Dalriada and the great Pictish lands to the east. Among Columba's triumphs was the conversion of the Pictish King Brude at Inverness. Columba's influence spread far and wide and has continued to do so down through the centuries. His influence lives on today in his hymns and his prayers and in the example he set for others, in particular among the monks of the present-day Iona Community.

There are, of course, many other saints who have an association with Scotland, for one reason or another. They include Saint Kessog (one of Scotland's early martyrs), Saint Donan (who may have been killed by Picts on the isle of Eigg), Saint

Did ye ken . . . ?

One of the traditional birthplaces of Ireland's patron saint, Patrick, is Dumbarton, which lies within the region of Strathclyde. When he was still but a boy, Patrick was kidnapped by Irish slavers, but he managed to escape after six years in captivity. He became a priest and eventually a bishop and decided to return to Ireland to preach the gospel. Interestingly, Patrick was never formally canonized, but that didn't stop him from being chosen as Ireland's patron saint.

Kentigern (also known as Saint Mungo, who is buried under Glasgow Cathedral), Saint Ebba (daughter of an Anglo-Saxon king and queen of Northumbria), Saint Cuthbert (who served as both a soldier and a monk), Saint Blathmac (cut to pieces at the altar of Iona Abbey by Viking raiders after refusing to hand over the relics of Columba), Saint Margaret of Scotland (who was born in Hungary but who married the Scottish king Malcolm III after being shipwrecked on the Scottish coast), and Saint Magnus of Orkney (in whose honor Orkney's great cathedral was built).

In the 2001 Government Census, only 67 percent of Scots stated that they followed any kind of religion at all. Of these, 65 percent were Christian, and of these 42 percent were Church of Scotland, 16 percent were Roman Catholic, and 7 percent were "other" Christian (including Church of England, Methodist, Orthodox, and Jehovah's Witness). Forty-two thousand people distinguished themselves as Muslim, there were more than 6,000 Buddhists, more than 6,000 Sikhs, more than 6,000 Jews, and more then 5,000 Hindus. Twenty-seven thousand simply registered themselves as "other." However, more than 14,000 Scots identified themselves as being "Jedi," which would suggest that the Force is strong in Scotland.

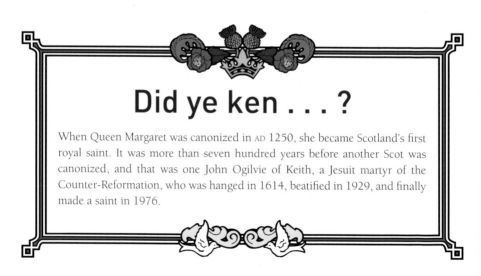

Did ye ken . . . ?

When Queen Margaret was canonized in AD 1250, she became Scotland's first royal saint. It was more than seven hundred years before another Scot was canonized, and that was one John Ogilvie of Keith, a Jesuit martyr of the Counter-Reformation, who was hanged in 1614, beatified in 1929, and finally made a saint in 1976.

WHY IS THE THISTLE THE FLORAL EMBLEM OF SCOTLAND?

The thistle is the official floral emblem of Scotland. You see it anywhere and on anything remotely connected with Scotland, with its prickly green thorns and purple crown-shaped flower head. You see it on boxes of shortbread and on book covers, and a stylized thistle even forms the logo of the Scottish Tourist Board.

"Thistle" is the common name given to a group of flowering plants characterized by leaves with sharp prickles along their edges and mostly belong to the family *Asteraceae*. But why should the plant have such a strong connection with Scotland in the first place?

The story goes that on a dark autumn night of 1263, during the reign of the Scottish king Alexander III, the Vikings came ashore barefoot at Largs, lead by their king Haakon IV. History is uncertain if they were intent upon a full invasion of Scotland, or whether they were simply showing their power by raiding the surrounding villages. Others claim that a fierce storm had driven many of their longboats ashore, and they were simply trying to retrieve them.

Whatever the truth of it, many of the castles along the western coast were on guard against such raids and a possible Viking invasion, as such a thing had been attempted before by the wolves from the sea. It was one such watch who heard the cries of pain of the Vikings and their leader as their bare feet walked on thistles. This alerted the Scots in time for them to see off the Vikings, thereby saving Scotland from an invasion and possible Viking rule. At last the role of the thistle was understood by the native Scotsmen and the plant was chosen as Scotland's national symbol and emblem.

The first use of the thistle as the emblem of Scotland dates from 1470, when an image of the flower was used on silver coins issued by the Scottish king James III. The thistle forms part of many Scottish symbols. For example, Carnegie Mellon University features the thistle in its crest. The word "thistle" is also found in the names of several Scottish football clubs, including Partick Thistle.

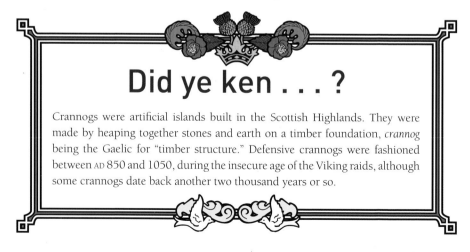

Did ye ken . . . ?

Crannogs were artificial islands built in the Scottish Highlands. They were made by heaping together stones and earth on a timber foundation, *crannog* being the Gaelic for "timber structure." Defensive crannogs were fashioned between AD 850 and 1050, during the insecure age of the Viking raids, although some crannogs date back another two thousand years or so.

Did ye ken . . . ?

The *Asteraceae onopordum*, commonly known as the cotton thistle, is also known as the Scots or Scotch thistle. However, there are other contenders for this title, among them the spear thistle, the musk thistle, the melancholy thistle, the stemless thistle, and Our Lady's thistle.

The poem "A Drunk Man Looks at the Thistle," by Hugh MacDiarmid, is an extended contemplation of themes which in part derive from the position of the plant in Scottish iconography. The song "The Thistle o' Scotland" makes use of the plant as a humorous metaphor for the prickly determinations of Scots.

In the language of flowers, the thistle is an ancient symbol of nobility of character as well as of birth. This is linked to the idea that the wounding or provocation of a thistle yields punishment. It is for this reason that the thistle is the symbol of the Order of the Thistle, a high chivalric order of Scotland.

It was James II (or James VII of Scotland, if you prefer) who founded the Most Ancient and Most Noble Order of The Thistle in 1687. It consisted of himself, as sovereign, and sixteen knights and ladies, as well as certain so-called extra knights, which included members of the British royal family as well as foreign monarchs! Their motto was *Nemo me impune lacessit* which translates as "No one harms me without punishment," but which is more commonly translated to Auld Scots as *"Wha daurs meddle wi me"* (which basically means "No one messes with me and gets away with it").

Did ye ken . . . ?

Carduus is the Latin name for a thistle, and *Cardonnacum* is the Latin term for a place festooned with thistles. This is believed to be the origin of name of the Burgundy village of Chardonnay, Saône-et-Loire, which in turn is thought to be where the famous Chardonnay grape variety originated.

This motto also appears on the Royal Coat of Arms of the United Kingdom for use in Scotland, and on some pound coins. It is also the motto of the Royal Regiment of Scotland, the Scots Guards, and the Royal Scots Dragoon Guards. Appropriately enough, the patron saint of the Order is Saint Andrew.

The Order still exists today, and only the sovereign may grant membership. Included among its membership are both His Royal Highness the Duke of Edinburgh and Princess Anne, the Princess Royal. Most British orders of chivalry cover the whole of the United Kingdom, but the Order of the Thistle is unique to Scotland, just as the Most Noble Order of the Garter is to England and the Most Illustrious Order of St Patrick is to Ireland (although this has now fallen dormant since its last knight died back in 1974).

Did ye ken . . . ?

When he founded the Order of the Thistle in 1687, James II claimed that he was actually reviving an earlier Order. According to one legend, the Scottish king Angus saw the cross of Saint Andrew in the sky while engaged in battle with the Saxon king Aethelstan. After winning the battle, Achaius is supposed to have established the Order of the Thistle, dedicating it to the saint, in the year AD 786. However, this hardly seems likely, as Angus and Aethelstan weren't even alive in the same century. According to another legend Achaius founded the Order in AD 809 to commemorate an alliance with the Emperor Charlemagne. This is possible, since it is known that Charlemagne employed Scottish bodyguards. Another tradition claims that the order was instituted, or at least reinstituted, on the battlefield of Bannockburn, by Robert the Bruce.

Women, other than reigning queens, were originally excluded from the Order, but in 1937 George VI (father of the current Queen Elizabeth II) made his wife Elizabeth Bowes-Lyon a Lady of the Thistle, thanks to a special statute, and in 1987 Elizabeth II allowed the regular admission of women to both the Order of the Thistle and the Order of the Garter. Knights and Ladies of the Thistle may also be admitted to the Order of the Garter. The Order has five officers: the dean (normally a cleric of the Church of Scotland), the chancellor, the usher, the Lord Lyon king of arms, and the secretary.

For the Order's great occasions, such as its annual service held each June or July, as well as for coronations, the knights and ladies wear an elaborate costume that consists of the following:

The mantle—a green robe, lined with white taffeta and tied with green and gold tassels, that is worn over the top of their suits or military uniforms. On the left shoulder of the mantle, the star of the Order is depicted.

The hat—made of black velvet and plumed with white feathers with a black egret or heron's top in the middle.

The collar—made of gold and depicting thistles and sprigs of rue, worn over the mantle.

The Saint Andrew—also called the badge-appendant, this is worn suspended from the collar. It is made up of a gold enameled depiction of Saint Andrew, wearing a green gown and purple coat, holding a white saltire cross. Gold rays of glory are shown emanating from the saint's head.

When a knight or lady of the Order dies, his or her insignia must be returned to the Central Chancery of the Orders of Knighthood. However, the badge and star are returned in person to the sovereign by the nearest of the deceased's relatives.

When the modern Order was created in 1687, King James instructed that the Abbey Church at the Palace of Holyrood House be converted to a chapel for the Order of the Thistle. However, James was deposed by 1688 and, during rioting, the chapel was destroyed. The Order did not have a chapel until 1911, when one was finally added onto St Giles High Kirk in Edinburgh (also known as St Giles' Cathedral). Each year, the queen spends a week at the Palace of Holyrood House in either June or July, during which time a service for the Order is held. Any new knights or ladies are installed at one of these annual services.

The Thistle Chapel only has just enough room for the sixteen Knights of the Thistle to meet in assembly with the sovereign and the officers of the Order. It is full of heraldic symbolism. Each member of the Order has his or her own stall, above which his or her heraldic devices are displayed.

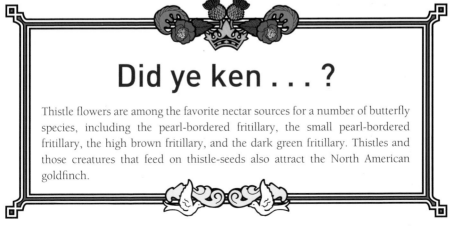

Did ye ken . . . ?

Thistle flowers are among the favorite nectar sources for a number of butterfly species, including the pearl-bordered fritillary, the small pearl-bordered fritillary, the high brown fritillary, and the dark green fritillary. Thistles and those creatures that feed on thistle-seeds also attract the North American goldfinch.

A 87

Caol Loch Aillse	1^1_2
Am Ploc	7
Balle Mac Ara	5
An Gearasdan	78
Inbhir Nis	85

WHAT IS GAELIC?

Y ou may be surprised to learn that Scottish Gaelic is actually one of six modern Celtic languages. Scottish Gaelic—along with Irish and Manx—belongs to the Gaelic group of Celtic languages, whereas Welsh, Breton, and Cornish all belong to the British group of Celtic languages.

Gaelic is named after a tribe called the Gaels who invaded modern-day Scotland (then called Pictland) from Ireland in the fifth century AD and settled there. This means that Scottish Gaelic is actually a dialect of Irish, and it is the language that has been in longest continuous use in Scotland since it was first spoken there over fifteen hundred years ago. Differences in pronunciation between areas are common in languages, and Gaelic is no exception; dialectal variations in Gaelic can even extend to changes in vocabulary.

While Cornish and Manx have come close to extinction at the start of the twenty-first century, Scottish Gaelic, like Welsh, Irish, and Breton, is still a living, practical language. Indeed, most people will have probably come into contact with Gaelic, and perhaps even spoken a little, without realizing it. Many surnames are immediately identifiable as Scottish because they start with the Gaelic word *Mac,* which means "son." For example, MacDonald literally means "Son of Donald."

Did ye ken . . . ?

There are approximately five million people living in Scotland today, but only around 75,000 of them speak Gaelic, or, to put it another way, 1.5 percent of the Scottish population speaks the native tongue. Most of the Gaelic speakers live in the west of Scotland, especially on its offshore islands.

The highest proportion of Gaelic speakers per head of population is to be found in the Outer Hebrides. There are also large numbers of Gaelic speakers in the Highland and Strathclyde regions, while almost 10 percent of Gaelic speakers live in Glasgow. There are smaller, but nonetheless significant, concentrations in Edinburgh and Inverness.

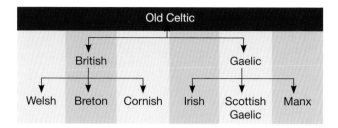

If you do not already speak Gaelic, you might like to learn a little of the language, especially if you have family roots in Scotland. And of course Scottish Gaelic has played an important role in the history of Scotland and its people. So here, just for fun, we present a basic Gaelic phrasebook and a simple pronunciation guide.

A Gaelic Pronunciation Guide

There are only eighteen letters in the Gaelic alphabet: A, B, C, D, E, F, G, H, I, L, M, N, O, P, R, S, T, U. On the whole the thirteen consonants are pronounced as they are in English, but with some exceptions. The sounds of consonants can be modified when joined with other consonants or vowels. Vowel sounds in Gaelic are short if they are unaccented and long if accented.

Consonant sounds

"b" is pronounced "b" at the start of a word but like "p" in the middle of a word.

"bh" is pronounced "v" but can be pronounced as "u" if in the middle or at the end of a word, and it can even be silent.

"c" as in "cat."

"ch" is guttural, as in "loch."

"chd" is pronounced "chk," with the guttural "ch" sound as described above.

"f" is the same as in English.

"fh" is usually silent but can also be pronounced as "h."

"g" like "g" in English.

"gh" before "i" or "e" sounds like "y" but can sometimes be pronounced "gh" as in "ugh," or can be silent.

"h" is a breathy sound as in "help" if it starts a word.

"l" is as in "hilly."

"ll" is like "lli" in "million."

"m" is the same as in English.

"mh" is like "v," or "u," or is sometimes silent in the middle of a word.

"n" is the same as in English.

"ng" as in "linger."

"nn" is like "ni" in "dominion."

"p" is the same as in English.

"ph" sounds like "f."

"r" is rolled.

"s" is the same as "s" in English unless it comes before an "i" or an "e" when it is pronounced "sh."

"sh" sounds like "h."

"t" is softer than the English "t."

"th" is either silent or pronounced like "h."

Short vowel sounds

"a" as in "cat."

"a" as in "sofa."

"e" as in "set."

"e" as in "late."

"i" as in "milk."

Long vowel sounds

"à" is "a" as in "far."

"è" as in "where"

"é" as in "stair."

"ì" as in "tree."

"ò" as in "lord."

"ó" as in "more."

"ù" is "oo" as in "fool."

A Gaelic Phrasebook

Some famous Scottish places	
Scotland	Alba
Glasgow	Glaschu
Edinburgh	Dùn Eideann
Inverness	Inbhir Nis
Argyll	Earra-Ghaidheal
Lochaber	Loch Abar
Skye	An t-Eilean Sgitheanach
Glenshee	Gleann Sidh
The Cairngorms	Am Monadh Ruadh

Some famous Scottish places	
Glencoe	Gleann Comhan
Loch Lomond	Loch Laomainn
Loch Tay	Loch Tatha
Loch Ness	Loch Nis

Days of the week

Monday	Di-luain
Tuesday	Di-màirt
Wednesday	Di-ceudain
Thursday	Di-daoin
Friday	Di-h-aoine
Saturday	Di-Sathuirne
Sunday	Di-dòmhnaich

Months of the year

January	Am Faolteach
February	An Gearran
March	Am Màrt
April	An Giblin
May	An Céitean
June	An t-Og-mhios
July	An t-Iuchar
August	An Lùnasdal
September	An t-Sultùine
October	An Dàmhar
November	An t-Samhainn
December	An Dùdlachd

Sport and leisure

sports	spòrs
leisure	cur-seachadan
shinty	iomain or camanachd
football	ball-coise
skiing	sgitheadh
hill-walking	coiseachd monaidh
mountain climbing	sreap bheanntan
fishing	iasgach
sailing	seòladh

Music

music	ceòl
bagpipes	a' phìob mhòr
harp	clàrsach
violin	an fhidheall
accordion	am bocsa
festivals	fèisean

Scottish wildlife

salmon	bradan
trout	breac
eagle	iolar
deer	fiadh

Some Scottish newspapers, such as the *Scotsman* (*An t-Albannach*) and the *Press and Journal*, as well as some local or regional papers, such as the *Inverness Courier*, the *Oban Times* (*Tìm an Obain*), *Stornoway Gazette* (*Gasaet Steòrnabhaigh*), and the *West Highland Free Press* (*Am Pàipear Beag*) carry articles in Gaelic on a regular basis. However, the only all-Gaelic magazine on the market is called *Gairm*.

There are a number of Gaelic words that have been assimilated into English and Scots, and some of the best known of these refer to topographical features. One of these words, "loch," has kept its original Gaelic form, but most others have changed subtly. "Ben" (a mountain), "glen" (a valley), and "strath" (a wide valley) come from the Gaelic words *beinn, glean,* and *srath.* "Bog" (a marsh) has its origins in the Gaelic adjective *bog* (meaning "soft" or "moist"). *Bog* is often used in Gaelic to describe damp weather. "*Tha i bog an-diugh*" means "It's damp today."

English has also adopted some other Gaelic words. One of these is *cèilidh*, which originally referred a gathering at which tales were told, songs were sung, and music was played. Nowadays a ceilidh usually means a concert of Highland music and song, or simply a barn dance, commonly held at the end of a day's wedding celebrations.

Of course men's Highland dress would not be complete without a sporran, and Scotland's world-famous Highland Games would be significantly less spectacular without the traditional Tossing of the Caber. "Sporran" and "caber" are anglicized versions of the Gaelic words *sporran* (meaning "a purse") and *cabar* (which is "a pole").

The word "slogan" that is banded about so readily by advertisers and political parties alike is thought to derive from the Gaelic battle-cry of *sluagh-ghairm*. Gaelic has also made its mark on the business world in respect of the names of prominent companies such as Cunard, the cruise line, which some claim comes from *Cuan*

Ard (meaning "high sea"), Alba Hi-Fi from *Alba* (the Gaelic for "Scotland," of course), Cala Hotels from *Cala* ("a harbor"), Skean Dhu Hotels from *Sgian Dubh* ("black knife," which was a ceremonial dagger), Craigendarroch from *Creag an Daraich* ("rock of the oak tree"), and Claymore Dairies from *Claidheamh Mòr* (meaning "great sword").

A number of Gaelic names have been adopted by English, and are now common Scottish names. Some, such as Calum and Catriona, retain their Gaelic form, while others, such as Hamish and Innes, are English representations of the original Gaelic names (*Seumas* and *Aonghas*).

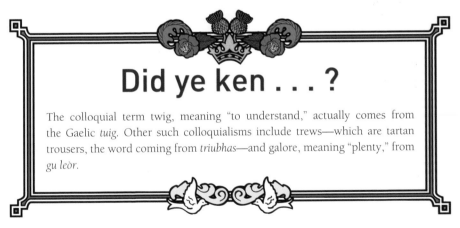

Did ye ken . . . ?

The colloquial term twig, meaning "to understand," actually comes from the Gaelic *tuig*. Other such colloquialisms include trews—which are tartan trousers, the word coming from *triubhas*—and galore, meaning "plenty," from *gu leòr*.

If you have enjoyed this brief foray into the language of the Gaels and you would like to find out more, there are plenty of accessible Gaelic language guides and dictionaries on the market.

You should be careful not to confuse Scottish Gaelic with Scots. Neither should Scots simply be dismissed as a dialect of English. Thanks to an EU ruling, Scots has been ratified as its own unique language. Common Scots words that you may have heard in common usage before include *tae* (meaning "to"), *wee* ("little"), *gey* ("very"), *ken* "know," *wadne* ("would not"), *kirk* ("church"), *bairn* ("child"), *aye* ("yes"), and *burn* ("a stream"). Scots speakers really do say, "Och aye the noo." It means "Oh yes, just now."

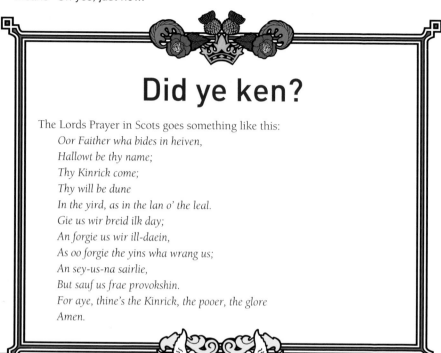

Did ye ken?

The Lords Prayer in Scots goes something like this:

Oor Faither wha bides in heiven,
Hallowt be thy name;
Thy Kinrick come;
Thy will be dune
In the yird, as in the lan o' the leal.
Gie us wir breid ilk day;
An forgie us wir ill-daein,
As oo forgie the yins wha wrang us;
An sey-us-na sairlie,
But sauf us frae provokshin.
For aye, thine's the Kinrick, the pooer, the glore
Amen.

WHO WAS THE REAL MACBETH?

*T*he Tragedy of Macbeth (or the Scottish Play, as it is referred to in theatrical circles) is one of William Shakespeare's most famous and most popular works for the stage. Thanks to his efforts, most people have heard of the Scottish king of the same name. Who was the real Macbeth? Did he really consort with witches and commit murder to secure the crown of Scotland?

Macbeth, or *Mac Bethad mac Findláech* (to give him his true Scots name), ruled Scotland for seventeen years, from 1040 to 1057, but it was William Shakespeare's play, written some 550 years later, that gave him his reputation as an infamous mass murderer. The Gaelic *Mac Bethad* actually means the "Son of Life"!

In Shakespeare's version of his life story, having won great victories against invading armies from both Ireland and Norway, Macbeth and his friend Banquo meet three very weird sisters who prophesy that Macbeth shall become king. Macbeth tells his wife about the prophecy. Goaded by his wife, Macbeth murders King Duncan while the old man is sleeping and takes the crown in what is effectively a military coup. His reign is brief and bloody. Along the way he has his best friend Banquo murdered, along with the entire family of his rival Macduff. However, in the end, Malcolm, Duncan's son and the rightful heir to the Scottish throne, returns to Scotland, supported by the English army, and lays siege to Macbeth's castle. Macduff eventually kills Macbeth and peace is restored.

He may have been—and, many would argue, still is—England's greatest ever playwright, but apart from the names of some of the characters, about the only thing Shakespeare got right in his retelling of the story was that Macbeth *was* king of Scotland and Malcolm did eventually follow him on the throne, although not immediately. Other than that, Shakespeare got precious few of the facts straight.

In reality, Macbeth was one of the better early Scottish kings. He brought peace to Scotland in violent times, and he was an effective and popular ruler. He was the

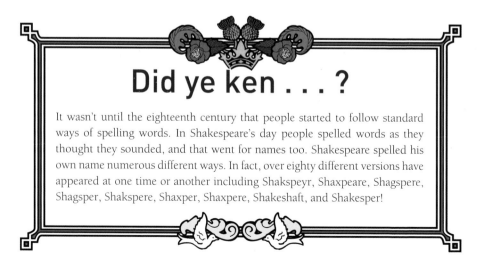

Did ye ken . . . ?

It wasn't until the eighteenth century that people started to follow standard ways of spelling words. In Shakespeare's day people spelled words as they thought they sounded, and that went for names too. Shakespeare spelled his own name numerous different ways. In fact, over eighty different versions have appeared at one time or another including Shakspeyr, Shaxpeare, Shagspere, Shagsper, Shakspere, Shaxper, Shaxpere, Shakeshaft, and Shakesper!

Did ye ken . . . ?

Macbeth wasn't the only Scottish king to be given a nickname. Malcolm III, who finally succeeded Macbeth's stepson Lulach in 1058, was known as "Canmore," from the Gaelic *ceann mor*, meaning "big head." Alexander I was "The Fierce," David I was "The Saint," Malcolm IV was known as "The Maiden" (since he never married), William I was given the much more manly honorific "The Lion," Robert I is better known as "The Bruce," Queen Margaret was "The Maid of Norway," John Balliol was "Toom Tabard" meaning "Empty Coat" (after Edward I of England effectively stripped him of his title), James V was "The King o' the Commons," James VI was "The Wisest Fool in Christendom," and James VII was called "The King o'er the Water."

first Scottish monarch known to have made a pilgrimage to Rome. According to Marianus Scotus, when Macbeth visited Rome in 1050, "he gave money to the poor as if it were seed."

It's true he became king by killing Duncan, but it was on the battlefield at Bathgowan, near Elgin, in Morayshire, and besides, Duncan was actually younger than he was at the time (twenty-seven to Macbeth's thirty-five). Macbeth did also lose the Battle of Dunsinane, but he didn't lose the kingdom at this time and didn't die until three years afterwards. He wasn't succeeded immediately by Malcolm either.

Macbeth (or "Red Head," as he was also nicknamed) was a nephew of Malcolm II and became one of the three kings that most dominated eleventh-century Scotland, although he was known as King of Alba at the time. He had already been Mormaer of Moray, meaning he was the hereditary ruler of the region and one of the highest-ranking nobles in the kingdom, the son of Findláich mac Ruaidri.

To understand how Macbeth was related to the royal bloodline of Scotland, take a look at the family tree of the Scottish monarchy reproduced on page 40, starting with Malcolm I:

In 1052, Macbeth was involved indirectly in the strife in the Kingdom of England between Godwin, Earl of Wessex, and Edward the Confessor, when he received a number of Norman exiles from England in his court, perhaps becoming the first king of Scots to introduce feudalism, a Norman invention, to Scotland.

Following Duncan's death, his sons Malcolm and Donald Bane went into exile. Malcolm took refuge with his uncle Siward, Earl of Northumbria, and Donald Bane fled to the Hebrides. In 1054, Malcolm, with Siward's aid, invaded Scotland. A bloody battle was fought at Dunsinane in which, according to the *Annals of Ulster*, 3,000 Scots and 1,500 English died—a significant number of casualties and no mistake!

However, Macbeth survived the English invasion, unlike his Shakespearean namesake, for he was finally slain by the future Malcolm III on the north side of the Mounth in 1057, after retreating with his men over the Cairnamounth Pass to make his last stand at the battle at Lumphanan in Aberdeenshire. The *Prophecy of Berchán*, a verse history that claims to be a prophecy, has it that Macbeth was wounded and died at Scone, that seat of Scottish kings, sixty miles to the south, a number of days later. Even then, Malcolm didn't become king straight away. It was Macbeth's stepson Lulach who was installed as king soon after. Macbeth, meanwhile, like many feuding rival claimants to the kingdom at the time, was finally laid to rest on the holy island of Iona.

In Shakespeare's play, Macbeth's "fiend-like queen" is given no name other than Lady Macbeth, but in reality she was an important political figure herself. Her name was Gruoch (or Gruach in some sources), and she was born around 1015, the granddaughter of former Scottish king Kenneth II. When she married Macbeth she was already a widow and had a son, Lulach, whose father was Gillacomgan.

According to the *Annals of Ulster*, Findláech, Macbeth's father, was killed by his own people in 1020, while the *Annals of Tigernach* have it that it was the sons of his brother Maelbrigde who committed the crime. One of these sons, Malcolm, died in 1029. A second son, Gillacomgan (Lulach's father), was killed in 1032, burned in a hall with fifty of his men. Some scholars have suggested that Gillacomgan's murder was the doing of another Malcolm, son of Cináed this time, seizing the opportunity to rid himself of a rival. Others argue that Gillacomgan's death was arranged by Macbeth in revenge for his own father's death.

If Macbeth was responsible for Gillacomgan's slaying, why then would Gruoch marry her husband's killer? The point is that Gruoch made a political match by marrying Macbeth. What she and her son needed was a strong protector. Under the circumstances, ironically, Macbeth fitted the bill perfectly.

Lulach's reign didn't last long. He is sometimes referred to as "The Simpleton" or "The Fool." After only seven months on the throne (although some sources claim it was as little as four months), he was ambushed and killed at Essie in Strathbogie, by the man who was soon to become Malcolm III.

There is, however, another mystery surrounding the identity of the real Macbeth. The *Orkneyinga Saga* relates that a dispute between Thorfinn Sigurdsson, Earl of Orkney, and Karl Hundason began when the latter became King of Scots and claimed Caithness as his. However, Karl Hundason is unknown to Scots and Irish sources and a common assumption is that Karl Hundason was an insulting nickname given to Macbeth by his enemies, from the Old Norse meaning "Churl, son of a Dog."

Bizarrely, there is a belief among certain scholars that Macbeth and Thorfinn Earl of Orkney were actually the same person, with "Macbeth" being a baptismal name. What is certain is that early annals and lists of the kings of Scotland call Macbeth the son of Findlaech; and Thorfinn surely succeeded Sigurd "the Corpulent" as Earl of Orkney. In other sources Macbeth and Thorfinn appear variously as allies, antagonists, and even half-brothers—although ties of blood and political ambition were not mutually exclusive in medieval Scotland.

No contemporary written source describes Macbeth as a tyrant. The *Duan Albanach*, which dates from the reign of Malcolm III, calls him "Mac Bethad the renowned," while the *Prophecy of Berchán* describes him as "the generous king of Fortriu," going on to say this of him: "The red, tall, golden-haired one, he will be pleasant to me among them; Scotland will be brimful west and east during the reign of the furious red one."

Although most of the important characters in Shakespeare's version of Macbeth did at least have genuine historical counterparts, there is considerable doubt concerning the existence of Macbeth's friend Banquo. It is possible he was even invented by an earlier fifteenth-century historian. In Holinshed's *Chronicles* Banquo is named as a Stuart ancestor. Shakespeare perpetuated this idea in his play, going so far as to make him a highly noble and honorable character indeed, in order to please his then patron, the new king of England James I. It's important to remember that William Shakespeare's play was an elaborate piece of propaganda. When he wrote the Scottish play, James Stuart had not been on the throne long, but he had been James VI of Scotland for significantly longer.

Of course *Macbeth* the play is notorious among the acting community for being unlucky. Those who work in the theater are well known for being superstitious and are great believers in not tempting fate in case things go wrong during a performance. For example, many actors believe it is unlucky to have real flowers onstage, or to

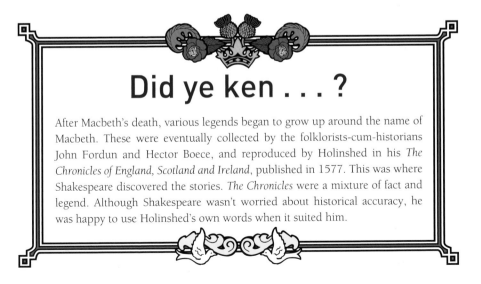

Did ye ken . . . ?

After Macbeth's death, various legends began to grow up around the name of Macbeth. These were eventually collected by the folklorists-cum-historians John Fordun and Hector Boece, and reproduced by Holinshed in his *The Chronicles of England, Scotland and Ireland*, published in 1577. This was where Shakespeare discovered the stories. *The Chronicles* were a mixture of fact and legend. Although Shakespeare wasn't worried about historical accuracy, he was happy to use Holinshed's own words when it suited him.

The Family Tree of the Scottish Monarchy 943–1153

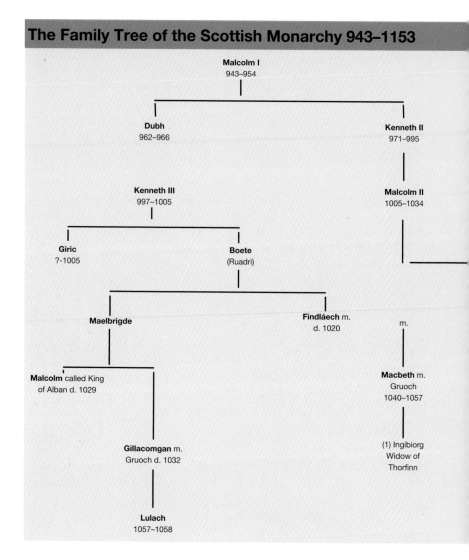

Malcolm I
943–954

Dubh
962–966

Kenneth II
971–995

Kenneth III
997–1005

Malcolm II
1005–1034

Giric
?–1005

Boete
(Ruadri)

Maelbrigde

Findláech m.
d. 1020

m.

Malcolm called King
of Alban d. 1029

Macbeth m.
Gruoch
1040–1057

Gillacomgan m.
Gruoch d. 1032

(1) Ingibiorg
Widow of
Thorfinn

Lulach
1057–1058

use real mirrors onstage, and claim that you shouldn't wish anyone good luck before a performance or even whistle in a theatre. When it comes to *Macbeth,* the play isn't just unlucky—it's supposed to be cursed! Why should this one play have garnered such a sinister reputation?

Probably the best known of the superstitions connected with it is that actors will not say the name "Macbeth" (whether they are onstage or otherwise), unless they are quoting lines from the play itself. Instead, they always refer to it as "The Scottish

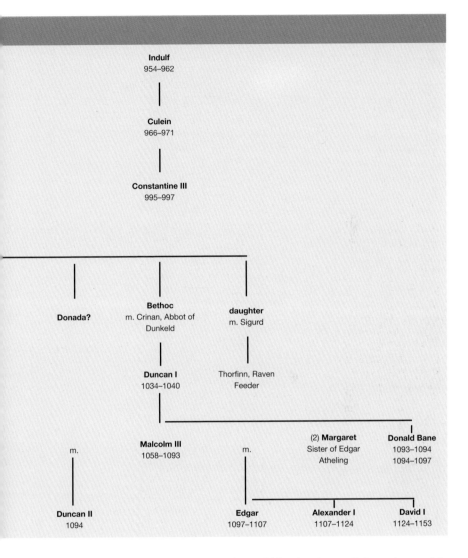

Indulf
954–962

Culein
966–971

Constantine III
995–997

Donada?

Bethoc
m. Crinan, Abbot of
Dunkeld

daughter
m. Sigurd

Duncan I
1034–1040

Thorfinn, Raven
Feeder

m.

Malcolm III
1058–1093

m.

(2) Margaret
Sister of Edgar
Atheling

Donald Bane
1093–1094
1094–1097

Duncan II
1094

Edgar
1097–1107

Alexander I
1107–1124

David I
1124–1153

Play." Particular lines to avoid are anything said by the three witches, since a fair number of their speeches involve magical incantations.

Actors who ignore this rule and who quote lines from *Macbeth* willy-nilly are said to be doomed, and will certainly make themselves very unpopular as their actions are supposed to doom the production as well. The traditional remedy for an actor speaking the name Macbeth in a theater, is that he or she has to leave the theater building, spin around three times, spit, curse, and then knock on the door to be allowed back in. Despite all this, the story goes that Sir Laurence Olivier, one of England's greatest ever actors, took macabre delight in taunting everyone he met upon entering a theater by greeting them with a flurry of quotations from *Macbeth*!

There is also a legend that the play itself was cursed because the first time it was ever performed, the actor playing the part of Macbeth died shortly before or after the production (accounts vary). It is also said that the original production of the play used actual witches and witchcraft, and so this is why the play is cursed, although, to be honest, that sounds like more propaganda and self-promotion than anything else. One particular incident that lent itself to the superstition was the Astor Place Riot, the cause of which boiled down to a conflict over two performances of *Macbeth*.

An alternative explanation for the superstition began in the old days of stock companies, which would struggle at all times to remain in business. Frequently, near the end of a season a stock company would realize that it was not going to break even and, in an in an effort to save their flagging fortunes, would announce a production of a crowd favorite to boost ticket sales and increase attendances. And that fan favorite was, of course, *Macbeth*. However, it is a tall order for any single production to reverse a run of bad business. Hence a performance of *Macbeth* often presaged the end of a company's season, if not, in fact, the company's demise. The belief that *Macbeth* was an unlucky play became self-perpetuating.

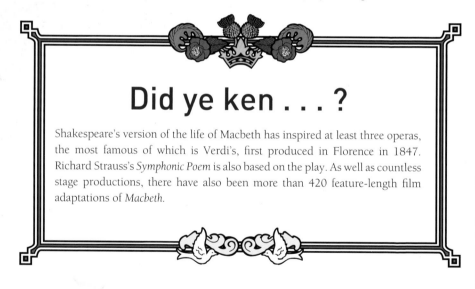

Did ye ken . . . ?

Shakespeare's version of the life of Macbeth has inspired at least three operas, the most famous of which is Verdi's, first produced in Florence in 1847. Richard Strauss's *Symphonic Poem* is also based on the play. As well as countless stage productions, there have also been more than 420 feature-length film adaptations of *Macbeth*.

WHAT IS THE STONE OF DESTINY?

The Stone of Destiny—also known as the Stone of Scone or the Coronation Stone—is an oblong block of red sandstone that has been revered of a holy relic for centuries. It measures 26 inches long, 16 inches wide, and 11 inches high and weighs approximately 336 pounds (or 152 kilograms). On the top of the stone the marks made by a chisel are clearly visible, and its only true decoration is described as a Latin cross. At each end of the stone there is an iron ring, supposedly added to aid in transporting it.

The stone was once kept at what is now the ruined abbey in Scone, near Perth. It was important to the Scots people, because it was used for centuries in the coronation ceremony of the monarchs of Scotland. It has also been used at the coronations of various English monarchs and, more recently, British monarchs.

Chapter 28 of Genesis tells how Jacob, one of the Patriarchs of Judaism, fled his homeland in shame, having stolen both his brother Esau's birthright and his father Isaac's blessing. As he was traveling through the wilderness, making for the land of Haran, the home of his uncle Laban, Jacob fell asleep, resting his head on a pillow of stone. It is then that he dreams of angels descending to the earth from heaven and returning again via a staircase joining the two that we now know as Jacob's Ladder.

According to the legend of Scota—the fabled mother of the Scottish race—the Egyptian princess herself brought this self-same stone with her from Egypt to Ireland, where it was set up at Tara, the ancient capital of Ireland. In time it made it across the sea to Pictland. It is due to this alleged connection that the Stone of Destiny has sometimes been known as the Jacob's Pillow Stone, the Tanist Stone, and, in Scottish Gaelic, the *Lia Fáili*. However, the writer Sir Compton Mackenzie believed that it had, in fact, been quarried in the Oban area of Scotland.

For 1,500 years, the Stone of Destiny caused no end of trouble for Scotland and its rulers. The Scots believed that any man who would be king of their country should be crowned while sitting on the stone at Scone, which became the capital

Did ye ken . . . ?

The last king to be enthroned in Scotland, upon the Stone of Scone, was John Balliol, in 1292.

of the Scottish kingdom in AD 840. However, King Edward I of England, the Hammer of the Scots, thought that Scotland should be ruled by him. As a result he actually had the stone stolen in 1297 and brought back to England, where it was installed in Westminster Abbey in London.

For the next seven hundred years, English monarchs (and later monarchs of a United Britain) were crowned on it. In the 1990s, the Stone of Destiny was finally returned to Scotland and placed in the Crown Room, alongside the Honours of Scotland, in Edinburgh Castle.

Or was it? According to one story, the monks of the abbey at Scone knew of Edward I's plan and so switched the stone for a replica. The English arrived at the abbey and duly took what they believed to be the Stone of Destiny and returned to their king in triumph. Meanwhile the genuine stone—you might say, the real McCoy—was carried off to the Western Isles, where it has remained until the present day.

Curiously, there is one event of historical record that might be seen as supporting this story. In 1328, Edward III made peace with the Scots at last and, as part of the Treaty of Northampton, offered to return the stolen stone. However, somewhat surprisingly, the Scots didn't want it back. Perhaps they knew that it wasn't the real deal after all.

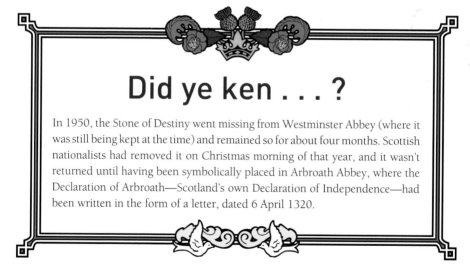

Did ye ken . . . ?

In 1950, the Stone of Destiny went missing from Westminster Abbey (where it was still being kept at the time) and remained so for about four months. Scottish nationalists had removed it on Christmas morning of that year, and it wasn't returned until having been symbolically placed in Arbroath Abbey, where the Declaration of Arbroath—Scotland's own Declaration of Independence—had been written in the form of a letter, dated 6 April 1320.

WHY IS WILLIAM WALLACE A NATIONAL HERO TO THE SCOTS?

Many people have heard of William Wallace and his struggle for national independence thanks to the movie *Braveheart,* directed by and starring Mel Gibson. What was it about this one man that made him the focus of the resistance against English rule in Scotland? When so many other famous leaders have risen and fallen since to fight the cause, what is it about William Wallace's legend that has made it so enduring?

For much of the thirteenth century, Scotland was a strong and stable country, ruled by the Canmore dynasty descended from Malcolm "Big Head" Canmore himself. This line of kings had extended their control into Argyll and Caithness, driving the Viking settlers out of the Western Isles. A link was forged with England in 1251 when King Alexander III married Margaret, the daughter of the then English king Henry III.

Alexander died in 1286, the last male of the Canmore line, his only heir his infant granddaughter Margaret, who also died while voyaging across the sea to her new realm in 1290, and suddenly, Scotland was left without a clear leader. The Scots decided to ask Edward I (who was by then king of England) to decide who should be their new king, and he chose John Balliol, a descendant of the great David I, believing that Balliol would help him secure the conquest of Scotland by the English.

However, Balliol rebelled and in 1296 Edward invaded. Balliol soon surrendered and was stripped of his royal insignia, earning himself the nickname "Toom Tabard," meaning "empty surcoat." First imprisoned in the Tower of London, then released into papal custody, he eventually ended up living in exile in his ancestral home of Bailleul in Picardy, France.

Just when it seemed that Scotland would fall into English hands at last, William Wallace appeared as if from nowhere, ready to lead the Scottish resistance. Born in 1270, the second son of a knight, Sir Malcolm Wallace, little is known about his early life since he did not emerge from obscurity until he was twenty-seven. In May 1297 he killed the English Sheriff of Lanark, William Hazelrigg, an action that was likely inspired by the murder of his father, his brother, and his wife by English forces.

Joining forces with Sir Andrew Murray, who was coordinating a similar campaign, in September of that year Wallace won a significant victory over the English at Stirling Bridge, defeating the forces of the Earl of Surrey and Hugh Cressingham. This was his finest hour, and he was granted the title of Guardian of the Realm in March 1298 as a direct result.

Now proclaimed the people's champion, Wallace recaptured Berwick, which drew many to the Scottish cause, and carried out other raids into Northumberland. However, despite his many successes on the field of battle, the nobles, whose support he desperately needed if the English were to be kept out of Scotland for good, remained ambivalent, largely because his social status was not high enough. These titled men were reluctant to fight in the name of a minor knight.

Unable to stand by and do nothing as this upstart Scot sent the forces of the English packing time and again, in the spring of 1298 Edward I, the Hammer of the

Did ye ken . . . ?

Following his victory at Stirling Bridge, William Wallace had an English cleric flayed alive and the man's skin made into a sword belt. More than five hundred years later, the infamous, but wrongly accused, body snatcher Edward Burke (he and his partner in crime William Hare were actually murderers, rather than resurrection men) had the cleric's skin turned into the binding for a pocket book.

Scots, traveled north to deal with Wallace himself. The two leaders met in battle at Falkirk on 11 July that year, and this time Wallace lost. In the face of such a failure, he resigned his guardianship of Scotland and traveled to France, at which point he disappeared into obscurity again for a time. While he was away on the continent it is known that he attempted to gain diplomatic and military support from the pope and the French king.

Wallace returned to Scotland in 1303, but by then the Scots' resistance had collapsed and he was only able to carry out a small guerrilla campaign. Edward I had set a price on his head, in the end Wallace was betrayed by one of his own followers in 1305 and handed over to the English.

He was dispatched to London by the governor of Dumbarton, Sir John Menteith, where he was tried on the charge of treason at Westminster Hall (now part of the Houses of Parliament). He denied the accusations of treason on the grounds that he had never acknowledged Edward I as king. The trial could only have ever had one outcome. He was found guilty and sentenced to execution.

Did ye ken . . . ?

In 1995, the movie *Braveheart*, which told the story of the life and death of Sir William Wallace, won five Oscars including Best Director for Mel Gibson, who also played Wallace in the film. *Braveheart* was good for the Scottish Tourist Board too, and Edinburgh Castle saw a record number of visitors that year.

Did ye ken . . . ?

The Wallace Monument, which includes an exhibit of Wallace's seven-foot (two-meter) sword, can be found in Stirling, on Abbey Craig. There are other, smaller memorials at Elderslie, where he was born, and near St Boswells. Appropriately enough, a statue of Wallace, alongside one of Robert the Bruce, now guards the gatehouse of Edinburgh Castle. America also has its own memorials to Wallace. The one in Baltimore, Maryland, is a copy of the statue at the National Wallace Monument, paid for by Scots residents of Baltimore and supplied by the same sculptor, D. W. Stevenson. It was unveiled in 1893, on Saint Andrew's Day.

On 23 August 1305, William Wallace was dragged through the streets to Smithfield and hanged before a baying crowd. He was then cut down before dead, disemboweled, and quartered. There was to be no Christian burial for the Scottish knight who had defied a king and led a country in rebellion against him. Instead, parts of his body were sent to Newcastle, Berwick, Perth, and Stirling, in order that his obvious fate might discourage other Scottish patriots, while his head was dipped in tar, to preserve it, and stuck on a pike atop London Bridge. It was an ignominious end for a man who epitomized the notion of Scottish nationalism.

With the figurehead of the Scottish resistance dead, Edward began to gain control of southern Scotland, and it seemed that the rest of the country would soon follow. It probably would have, had it not been for another national hero, the warlord known as Robert the Bruce.

William Wallace is celebrated today as a true Scottish patriot who emerged from Scotland's War of Independence with uncompromised principles and selfless motives, although his achievements have been somewhat superseded in the eyes of posterity by those of Robert the Bruce. However, there can be little doubt that his example inspired the Bruce, and the *Dictionary of National Biography* now acknowledges Wallace as being "the chief champion of the Scottish nation in its struggle for independence."

DID A SPIDER REALLY
INSPIRE ROBERT THE BRUCE
TO VICTORY AGAINST THE
ENGLISH AT BANNOCKBURN?

The legend that tells of how a spider, struggling to build its web in a draughty cave, encouraged Robert the Bruce to continue his struggle against Scotland's English oppressors is well known, by Scot and Sassenach alike. Did it really happen? And was the Bruce really the hero that history remembers?

Following the execution of William Wallace in 1305, Edward I considered his mission to gain control of Scotland accomplished. Fortunately for the Scots, two events saved Scotland once again. The first of these was the death of Edward I in 1307. His successor was his son, Edward II, who was a weaker individual and a poor military leader. The second event was the rise of Robert the Bruce.

Robert the Bruce's grandfather had claimed the Scottish throne in 1290 but had been passed over in favor of John Balliol. In 1306, the Bruce headed a new national independence movement in an attempt to promote his claim to the throne. He seized the throne for himself later that year after murdering a rival baron, John Comyn, at the Greyfriars' Church in Dumfries, and was hurriedly crowned Robert I, King of Scots at Scone.

The Bruce was supported by many Scots, who hated the English occupation, but the English fought back, and Robert was defeated twice. It is said that at this low point in his fortunes, the Bruce took inspiration from a spider sharing his hiding place in a cave. The notion of resolute persistence was well demonstrated by the way the spider was forced to climb up the wall again and again to build her web.

Did ye ken . . . ?

For over five hundred years, the story of Robert the Bruce's darkest hour did not include a spider at all. It is believed that the first reference to the arachnid came in Sir Walter Scott's *Tales of A Grandfather: Being Stories Taken from Scottish History,* published in 1827. The spider story was probably first written about the Bruce's ally, Sir James Douglas, in David Hume of Godscroft's *The History of the House of Douglas,* published posthumously in 1643. It is thanks to the Bruce version of the story that we have the well-known expression, "If at first you don't succeed, try, try, and try, again."

Whether the legend is true or not, following a period of soul-searching, Robert the Bruce resolved to wage a campaign of strategic guerrilla warfare against the English. Confidence in his leadership was greatly reinforced by his greatest military victory, at Bannockburn. In one of the most famous battles in Scottish history, the Bruce chose to face the English on marshy ground near Stirling in June 1314. His smaller army of men had dug and camouflaged pits. The English cavalry charge failed, their horses succumbing to the crippling pit-traps, and the knights were cut down by Scots pikemen. Despite being vastly outnumbered by better-equipped troops, the superior tactics and morale of the Bruce's brave soldiers won the day, with King Edward II himself forced to flee the battlefield in disgrace.

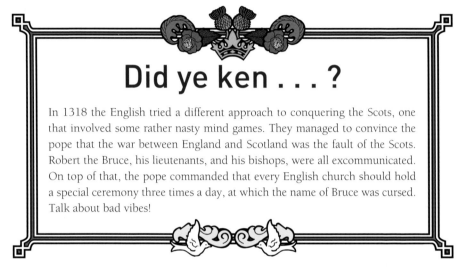

Did ye ken . . . ?

In 1318 the English tried a different approach to conquering the Scots, one that involved some rather nasty mind games. They managed to convince the pope that the war between England and Scotland was the fault of the Scots. Robert the Bruce, his lieutenants, and his bishops, were all excommunicated. On top of that, the pope commanded that every English church should hold a special ceremony three times a day, at which the name of Bruce was cursed. Talk about bad vibes!

The English army routed, Robert went on after this resounding victory to recapture most of the castles held by the English in Scotland, including Berwick Castle, and even began carrying out raids into northern England. Edward's grip on Scotland was broken. In 1328 his son, Edward III, was forced to recognize Scottish independence and Robert as king of the Scots, in the Treaty of Northampton.

During his reign, Robert made many legal and political reforms, but his continued popularity was mainly due to his concern for the rights of ordinary people. Now regarded as a hero of the Scottish people, rather than a murderer and an opportunist, Robert the Bruce died in 1329 (possibly from leprosy) having secured Scottish independence once again. Some even consider him the single most important figure in Scottish history. The warlike Edward III invaded Scotland several times in the years following the Bruce's death, but in 1357 peace came at last—at least for a while.

Did ye ken . . . ?

Robert the Bruce's dying wish was that after his death his heart be taken on crusade. His friend Sir James "The Black" Douglas fulfilled this wish, carrying the Bruce's heart into battle against the Moors in Spain. After the battle, it was found again on the battlefield, and returned to Melrose Abbey in Scotland, where it was buried.

WHY IS SCOTLAND KNOWN AS THE "HOME OF GOLF"?

*Q*uite simply, because the game of golf, as we know it today, is the descendent of a game played on the eastern coast of Scotland in the Kingdom of Fife during the fifteenth century. There are some historians who believe that the Dutch game of Kolven and Chole, from Belgium, may have influenced the development of the game, and the latter was certainly introduced into Scotland around 1421. However, while these games—like so many others, it has to be said—are basically, when you get down to it, stick-and-ball games, Kolven and Chole are missing that essential element that is unique to golf—the hole!

Gowf, as the Scottish game was once called, had the players hitting a pebble around a natural course formed from sand dunes, rabbit runs, and other animal tracks, using a primitive club. The first golf balls were made from wood, but in time these were replaced by leather ones stuffed with feathers.

Thanks to a newly gained royal endorsement, golf's status and popularity spread quickly during the sixteenth century. King Charles I helped to popularize the game in England. Mary, Queen of Scots, introduced the game to the French while she was residing in their country.

King Charles I was on the golf course at Leith near Edinburgh when he received news of the Irish rebellion of 1641. The first international golf match was also held at Leith, in 1682. Playing for Scotland were the Duke of York and George Patterson. The English team was made up of two English noblemen. The Scots won!

The first golfing society was formed there in 1744, to promote a newly established annual competition—the prize awarded at which was a silver golf club—and its members became known as the Gentlemen Golfers of Leith. The club was renamed the Honourable Company of Edinburgh Golfers in 1768, and a clubhouse was erected, although it was moved to Musselburgh, in Lothian, in 1836. The earliest rules of the game were drawn up in 1754 and included such classics as, "You must tee your ball within one club's length of the hole" and "Your tee must be on the ground." (Remember, it was still a relatively new game at the time.)

Of course one place in Scotland is associated with golf more than any other—and that's St Andrews. The first reference connecting the game with the town comes

Did ye ken . . . ?

The term "caddie" comes from the name given to the helpers of Mary, Queen of Scots, who were on secondment from the French military, known in French as *cadets*.

Did ye ken . . . ?

The Scots' enthusiasm for golf and soccer caused the Scottish parliament of King James II to ban both sports in 1457. The reason for this was that devotion to the game had resulted in the neglect of military training—archery in particular—and during the mid-fifteenth century, Scotland was preparing itself for an invasion from the English. This parliamentary ban was reiterated in 1470, and again in 1491, although people largely ignored it. In 1502 the ban was finally lifted, following the Treaty of Glasgow, and King James VI himself went on to take up the sport.

from 1552. In 1754 the St Andrews Society of Golfers was formed to compete in its own annual competition, making use of Leith's rules. Stroke play was introduced in 1759 and the first eighteen-hole course, which has of course become the standard everywhere, was constructed in 1764. King William IV honored the club with the title "Royal and Ancient" in 1834 and the now famous clubhouse was erected in 1854.

The British Open was one of the few sponsored events at the time, so most professional golfers were forced to actually make a living from tuition, ball and club making, caddying at competitions, and by betting against their opponents.

Did ye ken . . . ?

A "links" golf course refers to the type of soil and terrain on which it is built. A "links" (from the Anglo-Saxon word *hlinc,* meaning "a ridge") is any rough, grassy area between the sea and the land. The term "the Links" is now used to refer to any golf course. Of the ninety-two golf courses in Scotland, 17 percent are true links courses, and includes most of the historical courses. Another 10 percent are coastal with some properties of links courses and moorland vegetation. Apart from links courses, the other main types of Scottish golf courses are parkland (61 percent) and moorland (17 percent).

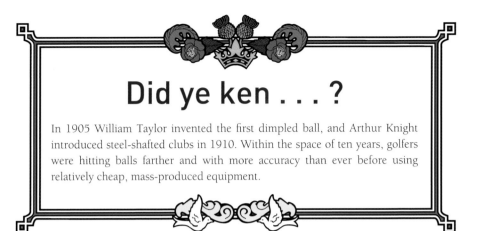

Did ye ken . . . ?

In 1905 William Taylor invented the first dimpled ball, and Arthur Knight introduced steel-shafted clubs in 1910. Within the space of ten years, golfers were hitting balls farther and with more accuracy than ever before using relatively cheap, mass-produced equipment.

The growth of golf as an organized competitive sport in the United Kingdom was paralleled abroad, particularly in the United States. The Saint Andrew's Golf Club of New York was formed in 1888, and in 1894, the United States Golf Association (USGA) was established to regulate the game in the United States and Mexico. Nowadays, as well as managing the rules, it also manages the handicapping system and even conducts research into grass. The first women's golf club in the world was formed at the Scottish St Andrews, in 1895, while the U.S. Open and U.S. Ladies Amateur Open were both inaugurated in the same year on the other side of the pond.

By 1900 there were more than 1,000 golfing clubs in the United States. Chicago was the first to have an eighteen-hole course. Unlike golf courses in the United Kingdom, which were typically links courses, American golf courses were often specifically landscaped parklands. In 1897 the United States led the way again, producing the first monthly magazine dedicated to the sport, called, appropriately

Did ye ken . . . ?

Other sports now popular in Scotland include rugby and football (soccer). From 1871, up to and including 2008, Scotland played England at rugby a total of 120 times. England won sixty-five matches as opposed to Scotland's forty-one. The two teams tied fourteen times. The first international soccer game took place in 1872 and was between—you've guessed it!—England and Scotland.

enough, *Golf*. Due to an explosion of commercially sponsored competitions across the country, the United States soon became the center of the professional game, although the most prestigious events were still considered to be those hosted in the United Kingdom. Golf was finally confirmed as a global sport when it was made an official Olympic event in 1900.

Today golf worldwide is regulated jointly by the Royal and Ancient Golf Club of St Andrews and the United States Golf Association. A summit is held every four years at which the two regulating bodes agree on any alterations to the official published rules of the game.

10 Rules of Golfing Etiquette

Of course there's more to golf than hitting a ball into a hole and trying to stay out of the water or the bunkers. There are centuries of tradition and etiquette to consider as well.

1. Don't take swings (even practice ones) when there is someone in front of you. It is bad manners and potentially dangerous; you might hit a stone or piece of turf at the other player.
2. Treat the green like a library. Keep the noise down, especially when someone else is taking a shot. A noisy group or individual is a distraction to other players. Also, mark up your scores on the way to the next tee, not on the green itself, making sure you leave the green as soon as your group has finished.
3. Don't waste too much time searching for a lost ball; it holds up play for your group as well as those behind you.
4. Always walk; never run. If you need to hurry, walk quickly but lightly, or drive your golf cart at a moderate speed. Anything more is at best distracting and at worst risks damaging the course.

Did ye ken . . . ?

The most famous golf shot ever played was by Alan Shepard, who hit a ball on the moon while visiting the satellite in 1971. He was watched by an audience of millions all around the world, and the club he used can be viewed in the USGA museum. Does this make golf the first sport in space?

5. Maintain a good pace of play and keep up with those ahead of you. Even taking fifteen seconds less between shots can cut up to half an hour off your total round time. To help achieve this, plan your shot while others are taking their turn.

6. If your shot throws up a divot of turf from the ground, always tidy up after you; put it back where it came from and lightly firm it down with your foot. You should also use your ball mark repair tool to repair the mark that your ball made when it landed on the green.

7. Only hit the ball when you are certain that the group ahead of you is out of range.

8. Always enter a bunker from the low side nearest your ball. Do not climb in from the top, as this will damage the wall, and after your shot, use the rake to erase any footprints. Leave the rake outside the bunker with the handle pointing in the same direction as the fairway to save any other player from suffering any nasty surprises.

9. You are not allowed to test the sand in a bunker by picking it up, or even by touching it with your club. The only time your club may touch the sand is during your stroke.

10. On the green, do not step on the imaginary line between someone else's ball and the hole, as you could cause a dent in the ground and destroy their chances of making a clean putt. Walk behind balls or step over the line.

The history of golf in Scotland is almost as long as the country's connection with horse racing, which has been popular for several hundred years. King James IV was a fan. One of the oldest racing events in Scotland was the Lanark Silver Bell, thought to date from the early seventeenth century. However, the race no longer takes place, as Lanark Racecourse closed as a major racing venue in 1977.

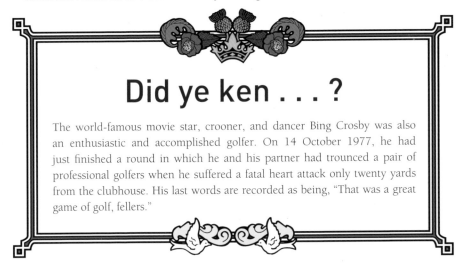

Did ye ken . . . ?

The world-famous movie star, crooner, and dancer Bing Crosby was also an enthusiastic and accomplished golfer. On 14 October 1977, he had just finished a round in which he and his partner had trounced a pair of professional golfers when he suffered a fatal heart attack only twenty yards from the clubhouse. His last words are recorded as being, "That was a great game of golf, fellers."

SCOTLAND

Foula

Lerw

Fair Isle

North Ronaldsay

Westray

ORKNEY ISLANDS

Rousay

Sanday

Mainland

Stronsay

Shapinsay

Stromness

Kirkwall

Hoy

South Ronaldsay

John o'Groats

Thurso

Wick

Lewis

Stornoway

Unapool

Lochinver

Helmsdale

Brora

OUTER HEBRIDES

Ullapool

Bonar Bridge

North Uist

Dingwall

Nairn

Elgin

Keith

Banff

Fraserburgh

Peterhead

Inverness

Portree

Stromeferry

Kyle of Lochalsh

Aviemore

Inverurie

South Uist

Skye

Aberdeen

Barra

Rum

Mallaig

Kingussie

Ballater

Braemar

Stonehaven

Eigg

Gulvain

Fort William

Kinlochieven

Coll

Tiree

Ballachulish

Pitlochry

Blairgowrie

Forfar

Montrose

Arbroath

Ulva

Mull

Oban

Crieff

Dundee

Iona

Inveraray

Perth

St. Andrews

Colonsay

Jura

Stirling

Kirkcaldy

Dunfermline

Dunbar

Dunoon

Greenock

Falkirk

Edinburgh

Eyemouth

Glasgow

Berwick-upon-Twee

Islay

Ardrossan

Kilmarnock

Lanark

Galashiels

Melrose

Port Ellen

Arran

Ayr

Hawick

Campbeltown

Moffat

Girvan

Lockerbie

Ballantrae

Dumfries

Newton Stewart

Stranraer

Kirkcudbright

WHY IS THERE AN ABERDEEN, A DUNDEE, AND A GLASGOW IN THE UNITED STATES?

The place-names of Scotland are full of mysteries, and one of those mysteries is why they can now be found all over the world. Although early written records about the origin of these place-names are few and far between, it is clear is that many of the names we know so well today have been around since ancient times.

The first mention of Scotland in any form of written record actually comes from Greek sailors, from before the birth of Christ. These early navigators sailed all round Britain—or Albion, as they called it—and probably landed in the area we now know as Scotland, speaking with the people living there at the time. The names they heard were reported back in Greece.

In the second century AD, the Greek scholar Ptolemy wrote a book about the geography of Scotland, giving names and positions for the *Orcas* (Orkneys), *Hebudes* (Hebrides), *Sketos* (Skye), and *Mallaos* (Mull), all well-known Scottish islands today.

The Greek navigators didn't differentiate between Scotland and the rest of Albion, and when the Romans arrived, calling the island Britannia, the people of the north still used the older name, although it corrupted to Alban or Albany. In later times the eldest son of the King of Scotland was given the title Duke of Albany.

An important document in the history of Scottish place-names is the *Life of Saint Columba*, written in the century after Columba's Christian mission to Pictland, by Adamnan, who was Abbot of Iona (as Columba himself had once been). This document is important because it provides us with the first written record of many Scottish place-names, including Loch Ness. *Ness* (possibly meaning "rushing") is also the name of the river that flows from the loch.

In the aftermath of Columba's conversion of the Pictish people to Christianity, and the subsequent invasion of the Scots from Ireland, the Gaelic language spread rapidly over the Highlands and most of the names in the northern half of Scotland belong to it. From Stranraer and Dumfries in the south, to Reay and Kinlochbervie in the north, every county contains place-names of Gaelic origin.

The names found in the Lowlands, however, have a mixture of Gaelic, Brittonic, and English. This is in part because in times past a northern form of English was the common language in that region. In the Lowlands a church was called a *kirk*. Kirkcudbright (which is actually pronounced *Kirkoo'bry*) is the "church of St Cuthbert."

There must be Pictish names in both the Highlands and the Lowlands, but the only Pictish word that can be definitely identified in any of them is *Pit*, meaning "farm" or "village." The name of Pitlochry means "the Pictish village among stones."

When the origin of a particular Scottish place-name cannot be explained, it is very easy to say that it must be Pictish.

Gaelic was spoken in most parts of Scotland from the ninth to the eleventh centuries, but many Gaelic words, such as *glen* and *loch*, are known in England

Did ye ken . . . ?

The name *Orcas* could have either meant "the island of swine" or "the island of whales," because in ancient times whales were sometimes referred to as "sea-pigs" (which just goes to show that the ancients must have understood that whales were mammals). The last syllable of Orkney—the "–ey"—is of Danish origin, meaning "an island," and was added much later.

as well. One of the most important is *dun*, meaning "a fort." As with other Celtic languages, the principal noun comes first and its description afterward. The many towns beginning with the word *dun* are easy to see on a map of Scotland, although in a few cases the "n" has changed to "m." Dumbarton was once Dun Breattan, the fort of the Britons. Dunkeld was the fort of the Caledonians. Dunbar was a fort on a hilltop, Dumfries a fort by a little wood, and Dunoon a fort by the water.

Fighting was a national pastime in the early days of Scottish history, and every chieftain had his own castle, often known by his name. The second parts of the names Dundee and Dunfermline are likely the names of early chiefs, although nothing else is known of them now. Dunblane is named after Saint Blane, who is remembered for starting a monastery at that location.

The spread of Christianity played its part in naming the land too. In Gaelic a church or holy place is signified by *Kil*. Kilmarnock is the "church of Ernoc," which could be named after any one of as many as twenty different saints, but who was quite possibly a relation of Columba, who went with him to convert the Picts.

Many Gaelic place-names are descriptions of the land itself. Most of the hills and mountains in Scotland have either Gaelic names or names derived from Gaelic, such as Cairngorm, which comes from *An Càrn Gorm* (meaning "the Blue Cairn"). Here are just a few other examples of familiar Scottish place-names along with their meanings.

Douglas	black stream
Glasgow	green hollow
Kilcreggan	church by a little rock
Melrose	bare moorland
Oban	little bay
Perth	a thicket

The ninth century saw the arrival of Viking raiders in Scotland. As well as bringing the fear of rape and pillage to the country, they also brought their language, which became absorbed into many place-names. These Northmen called the deep inlets and river-mouths of Scotland, not unlike those of their homeland of Norway, *fjords.* In Scotland this word became *firth*, and wherever you come across it now in an atlas (the Firth of Forth, for example), you can be sure that Vikings settled there. A narrower inlet was called a *vik*; this became *wick,* hence the ports of Wick, in the north of Scotland, and Lerwick in the Shetland Isles.

Most of the names on the northern Scottish coasts are Norse in origin, as are those of the harbors and headlands on the islands. However, the names of the whole islands have remained much as they were when those ancient Greek sailors reached them more than a thousand years before the Vikings.

The following are all elements of common Scottish place-names. Most are Gaelic in origin, as you would expect, but some are actually Welsh, or rather British, since the tribe that occupied the Lowlands of Scotland belonged to the same race that settled in Wales. They are presented here as their common anglicized forms.

Did ye ken . . . ?

Saint Cuthbert was a shepherd boy who became a monk at Melrose and was later bishop of Northumbria. In his youth he traveled the Border country and was said to have been beloved by all who saw him—including birds and animals. He had a special gift with the creatures of the wild. However, he isn't really a Scottish saint at all, but an English one, although he is barely remembered in the country of his birth.

Aber-	a river-mouth	Glas-	greenish-blue
Ach-, Auch-	a field	Inver-	a river-mouth
Aonach	a large hill	Innis, Inch	island
-an	little	Kil-	church, holy place
Ard-, Aird-	height	Knock-	a small hill
Balla-, Bal-, Bally	a farm	Kyle	narrow water
-beg	small	Letter	broad slope
Ben, Ban-	a peak, mountain	Lis-	court, royal dwelling
Bri-, Brae	hillside, upland	Loch, Lough	lake
Carn, Cairn	stony hill	Meall	lump
Carreg, Carrick, Craig	a rock	-more	great
Cashel	a castle	Pen-	a headland
Clack	a stone	Rath-	small fort
Derry	oak wood	Ros-, -rose	moorland or cape
Don	river	Slieve	range of hills
Drum-	a ridge	Strath	wide valley
Dub-, Dou-	black	Stuck	a rounded hill
Dun	a fortress	Tir-, -tire	land
Glen	narrow valley	Tom-	a round hill
		Tor	an imposing hill
		Tulloch	a small green hill

Why is there an Aberdeen, a Dundee, and a Glasgow in the United States?

Did ye ken . . . ?

An important landmark for the Vikings, who relied on the sea and their ships to carry them between the outposts of their watery kingdoms, was the northwest corner of Scotland, which they called *Hvarf*, meaning "the turning place." However, the name of this wild corner of the British Isles with its equally wild seas has been corrupted by English speakers to become the much more dramatic-sounding Cape Wrath!

The Scots have a lot of different names for hills, slopes, mountains, and peaks; when you consider the landscape of the Highlands of Scotland, that is hardly surprising. Of all the languages that have named the glens and lochs, the ports and forts of Scotland—whether Pictish, Welsh, English, or Norse—it is still the Gaelic of the Scots that named the most.

That still doesn't explain why so many place-names in such far-flung places as Alaska, Argentina, and Antarctica are Scottish in origin. For example, the Oil Capital of Europe, Aberdeen (once known as *Aberdon,* as it is situated on the mouth of the river Don), can be found in not only the United States but also South Africa and Australia.

One of the reasons for this is that in the eighteenth and nineteenth centuries, greedy, moneygrubbing landlords forcibly removed large numbers of Gaelic

Did ye ken . . . ?

It is thanks to the Vikings that the northernmost county of Britain is called Sutherland, meaning "the south land." The Vikings had colonies in Orkney, Shetland, the Hebrides, and the Isle of Man, and were all north of the mainland outposts with which they traded, which were, as far as they were concerned at least, away to the south.

from their homes in the Highlands and islands. Many of these dispossessed people were forced to emigrate, and Gaelic communities were established in parts of North America (*Na Stàitean Aonaichte*), such as North Carolina and Nova Scotia (*Alba Nuadh* in Gaelic). There are still many Gaelic speakers in Cape Breton Island (*Eilean Cheap Breatainn*) but the language is largely confined to the older generation. Many Gaels have also moved south to England (*Sasann*) in search of employment.

However, the Scots have always been among the most enterprising of colonists, and their names may be found all over the world. In the twentieth century, enforced exile gave way to voluntary emigration. Of all the groups of pioneers who ever left Britain, none have journeyed further afield than those who set out from Scotland in 1847 for the southernmost part of New Zealand. (The lengths some Scots would go to, to get away from the English . . .) Once there, they named their chief town Dunedin, which is the Gaelic form of Edinburgh. They did the same with their biggest river, which they called Clutha, the Celtic form of Clyde.

Scottish people have settled all over the world, from the Falkland Islands in the South Atlantic to Stuart Island in British Columbia. Wherever they have gone, they have taken their clan names and the place-names of the country of their birth with them as well, to the extent that telephone directories in Australia, Canada, and the United States are now full to overflowing with MacDonalds, Campbells, Bruces, and Stewarts.

Did ye ken . . . ?

Calgary, of the Canadian prairies, was named by a colonist after his boyhood home, which happened to be a tiny fishing village on the Scottish island of Mull. The name means "calf enclosure," and Calgary in Canada happens to be in the center of a cattle-raising district.

WHEN DOES A BROTH
BECOME SCOTCH BROTH?

cotch broth is a filling soup that originated in Scotland, as its name would suggest, but which is now obtainable all over the world. Sometimes called barley broth soup, part of the appeal of Scotch broth is that it is a little bit of everything thrown into the one pot to make a hearty, filling soup. In days gone by, Scots would eat it as a main meal, and even today it is commonly served as a meal in itself, rather than simply as a starter. It is particularly popular on New Year's Day, possibly because it was also regarded as being a health-giving soup with remarkable restorative powers.

The principal ingredients are barley, cuts of lamb or mutton suitable for stewing or braising, and root vegetables such as carrots, turnips, or rutabagas. Greens—usually cabbage and leeks—can also be added toward the end of cooking to preserve their individual flavors and textures. Dried beans are often used too. The proportions and ingredients vary according to the recipe or availability.

Of course, in this modern age of convenience food and prepared produce, Scotch broth is available ready-made in cans, but where's the fun in reheating a tin of soup when you could made it from scratch yourself? And the best thing about Scotch broth is that as with many slow-cooked composite dishes, it tastes even better when you heat it up again the next day.

Scotch Broth

8 oz. (250g) carrots, diced	8 oz. (250g) turnips, diced
2 onions, diced	1 stick of celery, diced
The white of 1 leek, sliced	3–4 oz. (75–125g) pearl barley
4 oz. (125g) dried peas,	
soaked for 4–5 hours	salt and pepper
4 pt. lamb or mutton stock	kale or other bitter winter greens, chopped

Soften the chopped onion in a little cooking oil in the pan. Once softened, add the water and the meat, and bring it to a boil, skimming off any fatty deposits from the top. After 30 minutes add the barley and peas and simmer for another 30 minutes. Add the remaining vegetables. Continue to simmer gently for a couple of hours, making sure that the peas become mushy and the barley expands, becoming soft and white. Ten minutes before the end of the cooking time you can add the chopped kale or winter greens. This recipe will serve 6–8 people.

Of course, another dish that is also a warming, hearty meal served in a bowl that is synonymous with Scotland is porridge. It is quick and easy to make and, of course, tastes delicious. In Scotland the traditional cooked breakfast begins with a bowl of porridge, eaten with salt, not sugar. Because it is made from rolled oats, it is a good source of fiber and helps to keep you feeling full after you've polished off your bowlful. It is even thought to help lower cholesterol if it forms as part of a healthy diet and lifestyle. Porridge is enjoyed not only in Scotland but also all over

Did ye ken . . . ?

The word "porridge" comes from the old Scots *porage*. Oat porridge was found in the stomach contents of five-thousand-year-old Neolithic bog bodies dug up in central Europe and Scandinavia. "Doing porridge" is British slang for imprisonment and came about because porridge was once the traditional breakfast in U.K. prisons.

the world, although the author of the first English dictionary, Dr. Samuel Johnson, wasn't a fan. He is quoted as saying that oats was, "a grain which in England is generally given to horses but in Scotland supports the people."

To make porridge the traditional Scottish way, you will need to use the finest Scots porridge oats or, failing that, a good-quality oatmeal. Soaking the oats overnight in the correct quantity of water needed for each portion will result in fluffier and tastier porridge. Some like to cook porridge recipes with water, others use milk, but you can use a mixture of half each.

Porridge

1 cup of oats
3 cups of cold water (or milk)
salt

Mix the oats and the water (or milk) in a pan and heat on a medium setting on the stove. You will need to stir continuously until the porridge has thickened, at which point you will turn off the heat and serve. And it really is as simple as that!

If you prefer to use oatmeal, especially medium oatmeal or pinhead oatmeal, you will need to simmer the porridge for up to half an hour, to ensure that it is thoroughly cooked. To give your porridge a distinctive nutty flavor, you will need to roast the oatmeal first. If you're after a quick meal, stick to Scotch porridge oats, which can also be cooked in a microwave.

There are a surprising number of myths surrounding porridge. One of these is that you should stir porridge clockwise while cooking it, otherwise the devil will claim the cook! The spoon used to stir the porridge was called a *spurtle*, which some people still call a "the evil," and in Shetland the porridge spoon is referred to as the gruel-tree.

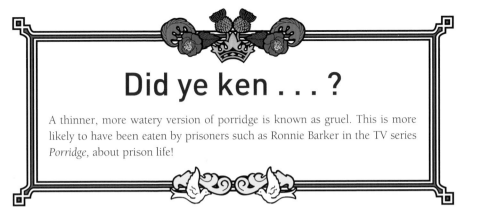

Another custom was that you should eat porridge standing up. Old recipes for the dish do not explain why porridge should be eaten standing up, but some theories have been put forward to suggest that it is an aid to digestion, or that the farmers and crofters who ate porridge to fill them up in preparation for a long working day were doing other things while eating porridge. These same crofters and Highland farmers actually had a specific porridge drawer in their kitchen, into which the remains of any cooked porridge recipes would be emptied. These leftovers were allowed to cool and would later be cut up into slices so that these slices of porridge could be eaten as a satisfying snack later in the day. These slices were called *calders*, and come the evening, they would be fried and served with eggs or fish.

The perennial question of what to add to porridge is always guaranteed to stir things up a bit. Traditionalists say salt, others prefer sugar. Some like to add milk or cream, while others favor syrup or jam. Many Scots have been known to add a wee dram of whisky or rum to their porridge. Other popular additions include cinnamon, berries, prunes, dried fruit, nuts, and slices of banana. You can even add stewed rhubarb or warm raspberry compote.

Celebrity chef Gordon Ramsay suggests using Greek yogurt, honey, brown sugar, or flaked almonds for alternative toppings, while the Jamaican musican and chef Levi Roots cooks a delicious Caribbean porridge that makes use of allspice, berries, nutmeg, cloves, cinnamon, coconut milk, tropical fruits, and pecans.

A traditional Scottish way of eating porridge is to have a separate milk bowl. Rather than poor cold milk directly into the hot porridge, the porridge would be served in its own wooden bowl and eaten with a horn spoon that was dipped into the milk bowl. That way the porridge stayed hot while the milk stayed cold.

The annual Porridge Making Championship takes place in Carrbridge, Scotland. The winner is the one who makes the best traditional porridge from water and oatmeal. The much-coveted prize is a golden spurtle trophy. Professional chefs take part alongside cooks from ordinary homes, and the event attracts many celebrities, including that year's Miss Scotland. The competition also has another prize for the best specialty porridge, which make use of ingredients other than simply oatmeal and water. To find out more about the annual Porridge Making Championship, visit www.goldenspurtle.com.

WHO WAS MARY,
QUEEN OF SCOTS?

During her relatively short life, Mary, Queen of Scots, made a big impact on Tudor Britain, and she left an indelible mark on Scottish history. Countless properties all over Scotland (including Glamis Castle in Tayside, Holyrood Palace in Edinburgh, and Jedburgh, which has its own Mary, Queen of Scots, house) purport to having had Mary spend a night or more there. Who was she, and how did her death result in the attempted invasion of England by the Spanish Armada?

The first thing to clear up is that Mary, Queen of Scots, is not Mary Tudor (a.k.a. Bloody Mary), sister of Queen Elizabeth I. Mary, Queen of Scots, was in fact Mary Stewart, Elizabeth's cousin. So now you know.

At the beginning of the Tudor period—at the time of Henry VII, Henry VIII, and Edward VI—Scotland was independent and thriving. Scottish kings were determined not to come under English control again. To ensure such a thing never happened, they turned to France—England's most powerful rivals—for help. This "Auld Alliance"—an offensive and defensive alliance—had been in effect since 1295, when the Scottish king John Balliol signed a treaty with Philip IV of France, if not in fact before. It had been renewed on several occasions since, but most recently in 1512.

However, a year later, war broke out between England and France, and the Scottish king, James IV, seized the chance to help his ally by invading northern England. The outcome of this invasion attempt was disastrous when, near the village of Flodden in Northumberland, the Scots were cut to pieces by a smaller English force, and James was killed. Peace returned for a while after this.

The new king, James V, however, was horrified by Henry VIII's split with Rome. He wanted to make sure that such a thing didn't happen in Scotland as well and so passed laws to ensure obedience to the pope. This pleased his allies in France, which was a Catholic country. Peace came to an end in 1542 when the aging Henry VIII (who was obese and barely able to walk) planned one last attempt to conquer France. If this conquest was to be a success, he had to stop the Scots attacking him from the north. In a preemptive strike, his army defeated the Scots at Solway

Did ye ken . . . ?

Mary's pet dog, a Skye terrier, went with her to the block, hidden under her skirts. When its mistress was dead, the dog emerged, whimpering. It is said that the dog refused to eat from that moment on, after which it pined away and died.

Moss. After Henry's death in 1547, the Scottish army was beaten again at Pinkie, in Lothian.

By now, James V was also dead, and Scotland's new monarch was his six-day-old infant daughter, Mary Stewart. When she was sixteen years old, she married the dauphin, Francis, who was heir to the French throne, thereby strengthening the ties that existed between Scotland and France. In 1560 Francis died. Mary, already a mother and widow aged only eighteen, returned to Scotland but found things very different from when she was last there. The Protestant faith had grown in popularity, and the Catholic queen found herself unable to keep control of her churchmen and nobles.

In July 1565 Mary married Lord Darnley, and the two of them ruled as king and queen of Scotland. This seemed a perfect match—they were both young, handsome, and Catholic; cousins, and great-grandchildren of Henry VII, with strong claims to the English throne—but in reality their union was a disaster. Darnley was spoiled and vain, and the Scots people disliked his arrogance and bullying. Mary grew to hate her new husband too, and grew close—scandalously close, in fact—to her secretary, David Rizzio. So enraged was Darnley by this situation that in 1566 he and his followers stabbed Rizzio to death, at Holyrood Palace, where Darnley and Mary had been married a year earlier.

Within the year, Darnley himself was killed, on 10 February 1567, when an explosion wrecked the house where he was sleeping. Many people suspected Mary of plotting his murder, with her new lover, the Earl of Bothwell, partly because Darnley's body was found in an orchard, along with that of his servant, nowhere near the scene of the explosion. Darnley was dressed in only his nightshirt and he and his servant both showed signs of having been strangled. When the queen married Bothwell only three months later, her subjects rose in revolt. Things had got so bad that in 1567, Mary, Queen of Scots, was forced to give up her throne and take refuge in England, under the protection of her cousin Queen Elizabeth I.

Elizabeth was not pleased to see her. Mary had a strong claim to the English throne, since she was the great-granddaughter of Henry VII, and Henry VIII had been her great-uncle. Her marriage to the French dauphin, albeit short-lived, had only served to make her an even greater threat to the English monarch. As a result, Elizabeth kept Mary under virtual house arrest in a series of remote country houses for the next twenty years.

Many Catholics in England and Europe wanted to get rid of Elizabeth, who was a Protestant, and they saw Mary as the ideal replacement, because she was a Catholic. She was also already queen of Scotland and importantly, unlike Elizabeth, she had already given birth to an heir.

Despite the fact that she had already proved herself to be a poor ruler (on her home turf), she became the focus for several Catholic plots. In 1569 some northern noblemen marched south with an army to rescue Mary. They were put to flight by royal troops, but two years later, in 1571 another plot was uncovered. To add insult to injury, Elizabeth discovered that one of the ringleaders was the Duke of Norfolk, one of her most trusted advisers. Norfolk was beheaded in 1572.

In 1583 government spies arrested Francis Throckmorton, who told them (having been tortured) of a French plan to rescue Mary. In 1586 an even more alarming plot was discovered. Anthony Babington, a wealthy Catholic, had arranged for Elizabeth to be murdered and for a joint Spanish and French army to invade England. This time, there was clear evidence that Mary was involved, although it has been suggested that Mary was set up. She was tried and found guilty of treason. In the end, after having put it off for as long as possible, Elizabeth signed Mary's death warrant.

Mary was beheaded in 1587, in the great hall at Fotheringhay Castle, in front of three hundred people. She didn't know she was going to be executed until the night before it happened. She went to the block clothed in a black dress, which she took off to reveal a bright red petticoat. The executioner needed three strokes of the ax to remove her head completely. After the axman missed with the first stroke, cutting the back of Mary's head instead, her servants heard her exclaim, "Sweet Jesus!" which was hardly surprising.

After the deed was done, Scotland's national flower, the thistle, was found growing in the grounds of Fotheringhay, and people still claim that it grew from the tears of Mary, Queen of Scots.

In 1588, the Spanish fleet arrived off the south coast of England, spearheading an invasion force, a direct consequence of Mary's death at the instruction of Elizabeth I. However, the Spanish Armada failed, and the fleet was sent packing. Ironically, a number of the fleeing Spanish ships were wrecked on the Scottish coast.

Mary was to have the last laugh, although it wouldn't be until sixteen years after her death. In 1603, as she was lying on her deathbed, Elizabeth I declared Mary's son as her heir. On 24 March James VI of Scotland was proclaimed James I of England, establishing the Stuart line of British monarchs.

HOW DO YOU MAKE TRADITIONAL SCOTTISH SHORTBREAD?

If you have ever visited Scotland yourself, you will know that every shop catering to tourists has at least a few boxes of shortbread on its shelves. You will often find that shortbread given as a Christmas gift (even though it should really be saved for the New Year celebrations that take place a week later) and also comes wrapped in packaging festooned with tartan, thistles, and images of deer roaming the Highlands, or scenes of famous Scottish landmarks. Why is shortbread associated with Scotland in particular, and what's so "short" about it, anyway?

Scottish shortbread evolved from a type of medieval biscuit bread that was made with yeast. In time butter replaced the yeast and the shortbread that we know today was born. Shortbread is a biscuit "shortened" by the prodigious use of glorious butter, which is what gives it its wonderful, melt-in-the-mouth texture. The texture of the biscuit is crisp and snap-able—hence "short," rather than elastic and "long."

The invention of shortbread is often attributed to Mary, Queen of Scots, in the sixteenth century, although it's possible that it was being made as early as the twelfth century. "Petticoat Tails" were certainly a traditional form of shortbread said to be enjoyed by the queen. The round shortbread was flavored with caraway seeds, baked, and cut into triangular wedges. The triangles resembled the shaped pieces of fabric that were used to make petticoats during the reign of Queen Elizabeth I. Shortbread was also made as individual round biscuits which were then, rather appropriately, called shortbread rounds. It also came as a rectangular slab, which was cut into thin pieces called "fingers." Unusually for a foodstuff that has such a long history, all these forms of shortbread are still made today.

Until relatively recently, shortbread was expensive and treated as a luxury item, reserved for special occasions such as Christmas, Hogmanay, and weddings. In Shetland, a decorated shortbread was traditionally broken over a bride's head before she entered her new home.

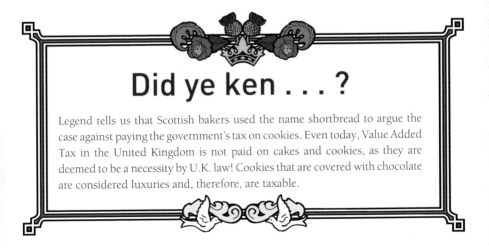

Did ye ken . . . ?

Legend tells us that Scottish bakers used the name shortbread to argue the case against paying the government's tax on cookies. Even today, Value Added Tax in the United Kingdom is not paid on cakes and cookies, as they are deemed to be a necessity by U.K. law! Cookies that are covered with chocolate are considered luxuries and, therefore, are taxable.

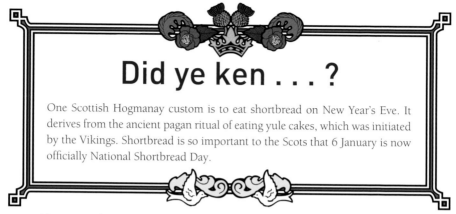

Did ye ken . . . ?

One Scottish Hogmanay custom is to eat shortbread on New Year's Eve. It derives from the ancient pagan ritual of eating yule cakes, which was initiated by the Vikings. Shortbread is so important to the Scots that 6 January is now officially National Shortbread Day.

However, shortbread has now achieved the status of an everyday favorite enjoyed in homes the world over. Traditional shortbread consisted of three main ingredients—flour, sugar, and butter—although the flour often has ground rice or rice flour mixed into it.

It is only in more recent time that the words "bread" and "cake" have been used to describe different things. For a long time, "bread" and "cake" were used interchangeably, because the cakes we know now were developed from sweetened, yeast-risen bread. Short*bread* is the descendent of the short *cakes* baked in the sixteenth century.

The sixteenth-century short cakes were made from the same ingredients that are now used to make sweet short-crust pastry (short here again refers to the texture) with the addition of a little yeast. This yeast could result in an uneven rise, which was remedied by the baker "docking"—or pricking—the surface of the cake. Some modern biscuits have kept these pricked holes, though their purpose now is purely decorative.

Short cakes were eaten across Britain, not just in Scotland, and many local biscuits—including Shrewsbury cakes and Goosnargh cakes from Lancashire—are variations on this basic recipe. Shortbread, however, has a definite association with Scotland, and the best of its type has long been an export from that country to the rest of the world.

There are as many recipes for shortbread as grains of sand on the seashore. While it is particularly associated with bringing in the New Year, it is certainly popular in Scotland throughout the year. Why not have a go at making some yourself, if you haven't done so before? You should find the following recipe straightforward enough.

Traditional Scottish Shortbread

5 oz. (150 g) plain flour
1 oz. (25 g) ground rice or rice flour

4 oz. (100 g) butter at room temperature

2 oz. (50 g) caster sugar and extra for decoration

Using a wooden spoon (or hand-mixer, if you prefer), combine the butter and sugar in a bowl until the mixture is light, fluffy, and creamy. Add the flour and ground rice and, using a round-bladed knife, form it into a dough. Use your hands to form the dough into a ball.

Flour a flat surface and your hands. Place the dough on the surface, kneading it round and turning it over, but avoid overhandling it. Flour the dough and the surface again, and form the dough into a round with a rolling pin until it is half an inch (1 centimeter) thick. When rolling, turn the dough 45 degrees each time it is rolled. This will prevent it from shrinking when it bakes.

Place the round onto a greased and lined baking tray. Using the back of a spoon handle, make slight indents all the way around the edge of the round, scoring it into eight segments using a sharp knife, and finally sprinkle it with a little more icing sugar.

Chill in a fridge for 20 minutes and then place in the middle of an oven preheated to 375°F for 15–20 minutes, leaving it to cook until it is slightly golden at the edge but still quite soft in the middle. When the shortbread is ready, take it out and cut it into segments immediately. Leave it to cool for about 10 minutes and then sprinkle with sugar. The shortbread may be served warm or cold.

Of course there are variations on this classic recipe, and some of these are peculiar to particular regions of Scotland. Ayrshire shortbread includes cream and eggs. Pitcaithly bannock has chopped sweet almonds and citrus peel mixed in with the flour, as well as being decorated with peel. Shetland Bride's Bonn is flavored with caraway seeds and baked on a griddle.

Below is a delicious alternative recipe with a few extra bits and pieces thrown in that isn't from any particular Scottish region. It is included here partly because of its festive connotations—in the nature of the extra ingredients—but mainly because it's delicious.

Cranberry and White Chocolate Shortbread

5 oz. (150 g) plain flour

1 oz. (25 g) ground rice or rice flour

4 oz. (100 g) butter at room temperature

2 oz. (50 g) caster sugar and extra for decoration

½ teaspoon pure vanilla extract

⅓ cup dried cranberries

¼ cup white chocolate chips or chunks

Make the shortbread as you would with the traditional recipe, only folding in the dried cranberries and white chocolate chips when you have beaten all of the other ingredients together. Then bake in the oven as above.

When it is golden brown, take the shortbread out of the oven and allow it to cool on a wire rack for 5–10 minutes before removing it from the baking tray and cutting into wedges. Allow to cool completely on wire rack before serving.

Other popular additions to the basic shortbread recipe include pieces of chocolate and stem ginger. Having made your shortbread, you might like to combine it with some other ingredients to make strawberry shortcake. To create this popular American dessert, simply serve a sandwich of shortbread filled with whipped cream and fresh strawberries.

WHAT ARE THE HONOURS OF SCOTLAND?

To put it simply, the Honours of Scotland are Scotland's crown jewels. Also known as the Scottish regalia, they date from the fifteenth and sixteenth centuries, making them the oldest set of crown jewels in the British Isles.

There are three primary elements of the Honours of Scotland. They are the crown, the scepter, and the sword of state. These three elements appear on the crest of the royal coat of arms of Scotland, on which the red lion of the king of Scots is shown wearing the crown while holding the sword and the scepter.

The crown of Scotland, in its present form, dates from 1540, when James V instructed John Mosman, an Edinburgh goldsmith, to refashion the original crown. The circlet at the base is made from Scottish gold, encrusted with twenty-two gemstones and twenty other precious stones taken from the previous crown. Freshwater pearls, collected from Scottish rivers, were also incorporated into its design. The velvet and ermine bonnet was also added at this time.

Historians of antiquities are not actually certain when the crown was made, but it does make an appearance in a portrait of James IV of Scotland, in the Book of Hours that was created for his marriage to Margaret Tudor in 1503.

The scepter of Scotland was given to King James IV, in 1494, by Pope Alexander VI. Made of silver gilt and topped by a finial with polished rock globe (which is believed to come from the Cairngorm mountains) and another Scottish pearl, it was remodeled and lengthened in 1536. One of several Christian symbols that feature in its design is that of Saint Andrew holding a saltire.

The sword of state of Scotland was another papal gift, this time presented to James IV in 1507 by Pope Julius II. The handle is silver and the blade is 4½ feet long. The sword is etched with figures of Saint Peter and Saint Paul, as well as the pope's name. The sword has a wooden scabbard, covered with velvet and silver and hung from a belt made of woven silk and gold thread.

The Honours have certainly had an interesting history. The existing set of Scottish crown jewels was first used together in 1543 for the coronation of the infant Mary, Queen of Scots. They were used again at the coronation of James VI, in 1567, and that of Charles I, in 1633. They were last used at a coronation in 1651 when the Scots, horrified by the execution of Charles I at the end of the English Civil War, crowned his son Charles II. Oliver Cromwell, the lord protector of England, Scotland, and Ireland (and leader of the parliamentarian forces that had overthrown the monarchy), was furious, invading Scotland and forcing it to join with England. However, by then Charles II had fled to the continent.

Scotland ordered almost all of the English regalia to be broken up or melted down. Seeing the Honours as the focus of kingship in Scotland, Cromwell tried to steal the Scottish crown jewels but he was thwarted because some bright spark had already hidden them—in a lobster pot, as it turned out—and taken them to safety, although the sword was damaged in the process. First they were taken to Dunnottar Castle, but when this was besieged by Cromwell's New Model Army, they were

Did ye ken . . . ?

The Honours have been on public display since 1819, with only one exception. In 1941, during World War II, they were actually hidden again due to fears that they might be lost should there be a German invasion of Scotland. They were not taken out of hiding again until 1953, when they were presented to the newly crowned Queen Elizabeth and then returned to the Crown Room of Edinburgh Castle.

smuggled out and taken instead to Kinneff Parish Church. Buried under the floor of the church, they were to remain hidden there for the next nine years.

Charles II eventually got this throne back, and in 1660 the Honours were recovered from their sanctuary. However, Charles never actually returned to Scotland, despite all the support the Scots had shown him in his time of need. Instead he remained in England, having a good time and earning himself the title of the Merry Monarch, and, once again, the Scots felt that their English king was ignoring them.

With the monarch absent, up until the Act of Union, of 1707, the Honours of Scotland were taken to sittings of the Scottish Parliament in the king's stead. After the Act of Union, the Parliament of Scotland and Parliament of England were dissolved and the Parliament of Great Britain, which sat in London, was formed. The Honours no longer had any symbolic role to play and so were placed in a chest, locked away at Edinburgh Castle and duly forgotten about.

They did not come to light again until 4 February 1818 when a group of loyal patriots, including the celebrated writer Sir Walter Scott, received permission from the Prince Regent (later George IV) to carry out a search of Edinburgh Castle, which proved successful. Following their discovery, the Honours were put on public display in 1819. They were used again in 1822, on the occasion of the first visit to Scotland by King George IV.

In May 1999, at the first sitting of the devolved Scottish Parliament, the crown of Scotland was present alongside the reigning monarch. The same was true of the opening of the new Scottish Parliament Building in October 2004, and at subsequent opening ceremonies of each new session of the Scottish Parliament since. However, due to their age and condition, the sword and scepter are considered too delicate to be brought out on such occasions.

All three of these symbols of Scottish nationhood, together with the Stone of Destiny, are now on permanent public display at Edinburgh Castle.

HOW DID THE SCOTTISH
NATIONAL FLAG BECOME
THE BASIS OF THE UNION
FLAG OF THE BRITISH ISLES?

In and around the thirteenth century, around the time of the seventh crusade, while the English were flying the flag of their country's patron Saint George, the Scottish adopted the saltire cross of Saint Andrew—a white cross on a blue background—as the flag under which they would march to war.

In 1606 England and Scotland were united, King James VI of Scotland having been crowned King James I of England in 1603, succeeding to the English throne after the death of his cousin Elizabeth I, the last Tudor monarch. As the two kingdoms were united, so were their flags, which produced the striking Union Flag.

The English flag showed the Cross of St. George in red on a white background. The Scottish flag bore the white saltire, or diagonal Cross of St. Andrew, on a field of blue. The first combined flag was formed by laying the red Cross of St. George, with a narrow white border, over the white Cross of St. Andrew with its background of blue. Later, when Ireland also was united to England, the red saltire Cross of St. Patrick was introduced into the flag in 1801. And it's still there today, even though the union with Ireland was dissolved in 1921.

Saint Andrew's white saltire cross on a blue background gives the Union Flag its truly unique look. So striking is its design that the Union Flag has become an intrinsic part of the design of a number of other national flags, including those of Australia, New Zealand, Fiji, the Cook Islands, and the British Virgin Islands.

Although its correct name is the Union Flag, the British national flag is usually known as the Union Jack. One of the possible explanations for it being given this name is that "Jack" in Union Jack actually comes from the French *Jacques*. It was King James I who ordered the production of the first Union Jack. The term "Union" was used because England and Scotland were united in his reign.

The British national flag should only really be called the Union Jack if it is flown on board the royal yacht. "Jack" is actually the proper name for a flag flown from the jackstaff at the bow of a ship, but the Union Jack is only used in this way by Her Majesty Queen Elizabeth II. It is flown on the mainmast by the Admiral of the Fleet.

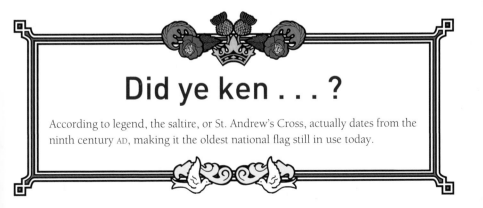

Did ye ken . . . ?

According to legend, the saltire, or St. Andrew's Cross, actually dates from the ninth century AD, making it the oldest national flag still in use today.

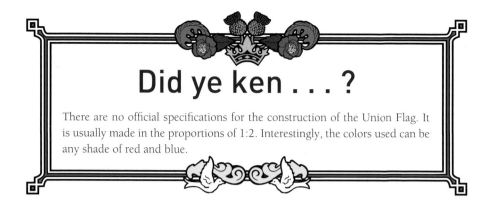

Did ye ken . . . ?

There are no official specifications for the construction of the Union Flag. It is usually made in the proportions of 1:2. Interestingly, the colors used can be any shade of red and blue.

The Union Flag is the national flag for use on land. It is also used by the Commander in Chief of the British Army.

The Union Jack appears in the top left-hand hoist corner of each of the three ensigns. The White Ensign has a field of white. This is the flag of the British Royal Navy, the Dominions' Navies, and the Royal Yacht Squadron. The Blue Ensign has a blue background. It is flown by the Royal Naval Reserve and certain merchant vessels with naval reservists in their crews. The Red Ensign (nicknamed the Red Duster) has a plain red background, and is carried by all ships that do not fly the White or Blue Ensign.

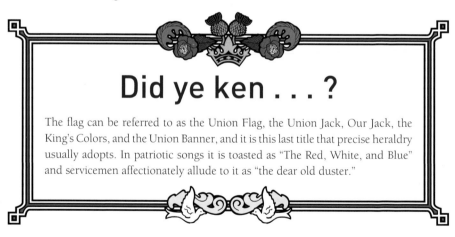

Did ye ken . . . ?

The flag can be referred to as the Union Flag, the Union Jack, Our Jack, the King's Colors, and the Union Banner, and it is this last title that precise heraldry usually adopts. In patriotic songs it is toasted as "The Red, White, and Blue" and servicemen affectionately allude to it as "the dear old duster."

WAS ROB ROY REALLY A
SCOTTISH ROBIN HOOD?

Rob Roy is a legendary outlaw from Scottish history; the tales of his daring, roguish exploits have earned him a status in Scotland akin to that of Robin Hood in England. Although we can be sure that he did exist, was he really quite the folk hero that he is remembered as today?

Rob Roy was actually baptized Robert Roy MacGregor on 7 March 1671, and his birth was recorded in the parish registers of Buchanan as follows:

> On the 7th day of March 1671, Donald M'Gregor in GlenGyle, ps. of Calendar, upon testificat from ye minister yrof. Margaret Campbell. Son baptised, called Robert. Witnesses, Mr. Wm. Anderson, Minister, and John Macgregor.

In later life Rob Roy was also known as Red MacGregor, because of his striking red hair ("roy" being a corruption of the Gaelic *ruadh*, meaning "red"). The reason he is still so well known today is thanks to the work of the renowned Scottish writer Sir Walter Scott, specifically the romantic novel *Rob Roy*, published in 1817, eighty-three years after the protagonist's death in 1734.

Robert MacGregor was born at the head of Loch Katrine in the Trossachs. He was born into a Protestant family, the third son of Lieutenant-Colonel Donald MacGregor of Glengyle and Margaret Campbell. Robert was renowned for his great strength, his exceptionally long arms, and his skill with the broadsword.

Rob saw military action in 1689, aged only eighteen, when he fought with his father under Viscount Dundee at Killiecrankie during the Jacobite uprising in support of the Stuart King James against William of Orange. Despite some initial successes, "Bonnie Dundee" finally fell in battle, and the fortunes of the MacGregor family seemed to fall with him. Rob's father was taken to jail and held on treason charges for two years. By the time Donald was finally released, his wife was already dead. Rob himself went on to join a group of Highlanders called the Lennox Watch. This body

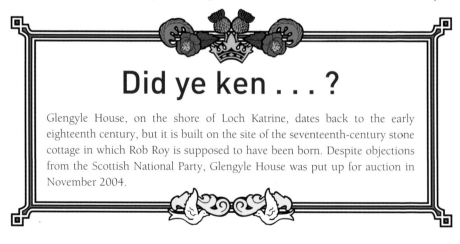

Did ye ken . . . ?

Glengyle House, on the shore of Loch Katrine, dates back to the early eighteenth century, but it is built on the site of the seventeenth-century stone cottage in which Rob Roy is supposed to have been born. Despite objections from the Scottish National Party, Glengyle House was put up for auction in November 2004.

of men protected the people of the Lowlands of Scotland in return for a payment that was termed "blackmail."

He married Mary Campbell of Comer, in 1693, and the two of them produced four sons: James (known as "Mor" or "Tall"), Ranald, Coll, and Robert (known as "Robin Oig" or "Young Rob"). They also adopted a cousin, Duncan. In 1694, when even the name Mac-Gregor became outlawed, Rob took the name of Campbell himself.

He became a well-known and respected cattleman, having acquired the lands of Craigroyston in 1701, and later those of Inversnaid on the eastern shore of Loch Lomond. He also rented grazing land at Balquhidder in Perthshire. In front of the east-facing gable of the old church of Balquhidder you will now find the graves of Rob, Mary, and two of their sons.

In the early eighteenth century, cattle rustling and selling protection against theft were both common ways to earn a living. Rob lost both money and cattle when he borrowed a significant sum (£1,000) to increase his own herd; his chief herder—a MacDonald—disappeared with the cash, the cattle never showed up, and Rob defaulted on his loan. A warrant was issued for his arrest on 3 October 1712. Because he failed to answer the summons, Rob was branded an outlaw. His wife and family were evicted from their house at Inversnaid, which, to add insult to injury, was then burned down.

Rob's principal creditor was the First Duke of Montrose, James Graham. When Graham seized his lands, Rob Roy waged a private feud against the duke, raiding the Lowlands from the Trossachs, but particularly the lands of Montrose.

In 1715, Rob mobilized Clan Gregor for the Jacobite cause once again but was badly wounded at the Battle of Glen Shiel (in 1719) which also saw the defeat of a Spanish expedition aimed at restoring the Stuart monarchy.

Rob's many daring exploits became the stuff of legend. He twice escaped imprisonment and even got away after being captured near Stirling, despite being mounted on a horse, tied behind one of his captors; while they were crossing the River Forth, he managed to cut the belt holding him and, plunging into the water, swam away. He finally submitted to General Wade and was imprisoned once more, but was finally pardoned in 1727. Seven years later, on 28 December 1734, he died at home at Inverlochlarig Beg, Balquhidder.

Rob Roy is commonly depicted as being a bit of a rogue, a heroic Scottish Robin Hood at best, and, at worst, an outright criminal. What makes the interpretation of his deeds so difficult is that life in the Scottish Highlands in the late seventeenth and early eighteenth centuries was very different from life today. At this time the High-

lands were still in turmoil, thanks to the Jacobite risings, and life was hard. In many ways life was cheap, and certainly people's values were quite different from those people hold in our modern age.

The world in which Rob Roy lived was one in which clan loyalties were still fairly strong and Scots Highlanders were generally reluctant to follow the rules imposed on them by outsiders, especially people from the Lowlands and even farther south. Cattle rustling (or "lifting" as it was known) was a way of life for many Highland clans and often the only way for them to survive. Therefore, the life and crimes of Rob Roy should not really be judged using our own, modern values.

As with Robert the Bruce's struggle and the persistent spider that inspired him to greatness, Sir Walter Scott mythologized Rob Roy's criminal activities. Before Scott ever got his hands on the story, a fictionalized account of Rob Roy's life, called *The Highland Rogue*, appeared in 1723. It was written by Daniel Defoe, the author of *Robinson Crusoe*, and made the outlaw and Jacobite supporter a legend in his own lifetime. It is commonly held that this account even influenced George I's decision to issue a pardon for Rob's crimes just as he was about to be transported to the colonies.

Scott turned Rob Roy MacGregor, the cattle thief, outlaw, and blackmailer, into Rob Roy, a Scottish rival to Robin Hood. Scott was the most popular writer of his age, and he reinvented Scottish history. He started writing historical novels based on Scotland's past, making it sound like it had been a glorious and glamorous time to live—even though in reality it may not have been quite so glorious or so glamorous. For the first time in British literature, Scots men and women were cast as heroes and heroines.

Did ye ken . . . ?

George IV was so worried that the wind might lift up his kilt, revealing his own crown jewels for the admiring Scots to see, as it were, that he wore pink tights underneath, just in case!

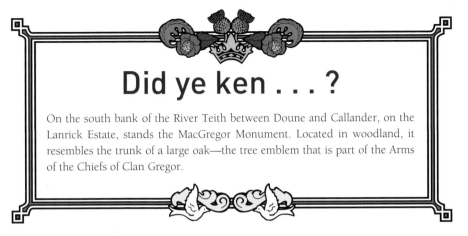

Did ye ken . . . ?

On the south bank of the River Teith between Doune and Callander, on the Lanrick Estate, stands the MacGregor Monument. Located in woodland, it resembles the trunk of a large oak—the tree emblem that is part of the Arms of the Chiefs of Clan Gregor.

Despite his habit of glamorizing the past, Scott's other achievements should not be overlooked. When Scotland became part of Great Britain the Scottish crown jewels were locked away. Eleven years later, Scott made sure they were brought out of hiding again so that the world might better understand the glory of Scotland's past. If it hadn't have been for Sir Walter Scott, the name "Scotland" might have gone the same way as Pictland, Alba, and Caledonia.

Scott organized a two-week visit of King George IV to Scotland. Chieftains and clansmen in new tartan met the monarch. The king even wrapped a huge kilt around himself and was cheered as "the chief of the chiefs." The Lowland tradesmen cashed in, selling miles of tartan to both the Scots and the English, even though many of the latter had never even seen a glen or set foot on a ben themselves.

Even the Highlands—the place that Rob Roy called home—became part of Scott's magical New Scotland. Where before they had been nothing more than a cold, bleak wilderness, now they were regarded as examples of dramatic, breathtaking, rugged, unspoiled scenery.

Thanks mainly to the work of Sir Walter Scott, Rob Roy's legacy lives on to this day. A long-distance footpath from Drymen to Pitlochry, called the Rob Roy Way, was created in 2002 and named in the cattle rustler's honor.

Descendants of Rob Roy also settled around McGregor, Iowa, in the United States, and in 1849 it was reported that the original MacGregor seal and signet were owned by one Alex McGregor of Iowa. The clan seal was inscribed with the Gaelic words *"Triogal Ma Dh'ream/Een dhn bait spair nocht,"* which is taken to mean "I am of royal descent/Slay and spare not," and the signet ring was a bloodstone from Loch Lomond.

Rob Roy also inadvertently gave his name to a cocktail, similar to a Manhattan, that first appeared in New York City around 1890. The Rob Roy is made with Scotch whisky, naturally, and owes its existence in part to the introduction of Dewar's Scotch Whisky to the United States, and in part to the premiere of the operetta *Rob Roy* by Reginald de Koven.

It is made with 1½ fl oz. (45 ml) Scotch whisky, 0.85 US fl oz. (25 ml) sweet vermouth, and a dash (25 ml) Angostura bitters. Stirred over ice and strained into a chilled glass, it is served straight up or on the rocks in a standard cocktail glass. A dry Rob Roy is made by replacing the sweet vermouth with dry vermouth, while a perfect Rob Roy is made with equal parts sweet and dry. It is garnished with a maraschino cherry, if it is sweet, or lemon twist if perfect or dry.

Did ye ken . . . ?

Rob Roy is the name of a small town in Fountain County, Indiana. The sportsman John MacGregor—responsible for developing the first sailing canoes, popularizing canoeing as a sport in Europe and the United States, and founding the English Royal Canoe Club (RCC) in 1866—was nicknamed Rob Roy and also had a boat that bore the same name. A football club from Kirkintilloch, Scotland, also bears his name—Kirkintilloch Rob Roy F.C.

WHEN DID THE LION AND THE UNICORN FIGHT FOR THE CROWN, AND WHAT DOES THIS HAVE TO DO WITH BONNIE PRINCE CHARLIE?

The lion and the unicorn were fighting for the crown,
The lion beat the unicorn all around the town;
Some gave them white bread and some gave them brown,
Some gave them plum cake and drummed them out of town.

So goes the nursery rhyme, famously interwoven into the plot of Lewis Carroll's sequel to *Alice's Adventures in Wonderland*, *Alice through the Looking Glass*. What (you are doubtless thinking) does this have to do with a book about Scotland and Scottish culture?

Like so many nursery rhymes, "The Lion and the Unicorn" is based on actual, historical events. In this case, it recalls the traditionally tense relationship between England and Scotland. England (represented by the lion) and Scotland (the unicorn) had been at odds with one another since the time of Edward I. Things calmed down for a while when James VI of Scotland became James I of England in 1603, and the two kingdoms were united under one royal dynasty—that of the Stuarts. Ever since that time, the Royal Coat of Arms of the United Kingdom has included both the lion and the unicorn in its composition.

However, the Stuart monarchy didn't remain on the English throne for long. Not one, but two Stuart kings were actually sacked by parliament and the people, and in 1714 the Hanoverian line took over. The Scots, of course, remained loyal to the Stuart line, even though they were technically supposed to be British citizens.

When Bonnie Prince Charlie—otherwise known as Charles Edward Stuart, or "The Young Pretender"—landed in Scotland in 1745, many rallied to his cause, which resulted in the lion (in the guise of Prince William, the Duke of Cumberland,

Did ye ken . . . ?

The usual Scottish spelling of Stuart (as in the Stuart line of monarchs) is actually "Stewart" or even "Steward." The name denotes descent from Walter, Third High Steward of Scotland. "Stuart" is the anglicized version of the Scottish-preferred "Stewart," which is commonly used when referring to the royal House of Stuart after 1603, when James VI of Scotland also became James I of England, which is why you will see both spellings in use in this book. The change from "Stewart" to "Stuart" is thought to have been a concession to the French—Scotland's and the Stewarts' *auld* allies—since their language has no letter "w."

King George II's son) and the unicorn (in this case, Bonnie Prince Charlie) fighting for the crown of Scotland for real.

On 17 September 1745 Bonnie Prince Charlie arrived in Edinburgh, declaring that his father was the rightful king of Scotland (his grandfather having been the deposed Catholic king James II who was forced to flee from the Protestant William of Orange's invading army in 1688) and, unable to capture Edinburgh Castle, set up his own court in Holyrood Palace. In Scotland, supporters of James were known as Jacobites (from the Latin for James, *Jacobus*). The final Jacobite Rebellion had begun.

Bonnie Prince Charlie and his Jacobite followers soon appeared to have gained the upper hand, winning important victories at Prestopans and Carlisle. They then drove south, invading England. Most of the British army was busy fighting the French in Flanders, and so contingency plans to evacuate the king to Hanover were drawn up. The Jacobites failed to recruit supporters in England, and the planned French invasion was postponed. By the time they reached Derby, Bonnie Prince Charlie's advisers pressured him into agreeing to return to Scotland, because none of the English support he had been promised had shown up. This left the Scots exposed and vulnerable to attack.

Did ye ken . . . ?

Although the Battle of Culloden is recorded in the history books as having been fought between the Scottish and the English, it was actually more a case of Scotland versus Scotland. It is interesting to note that there were more Scots in the army that defeated Bonnie Prince Charlie than there were on the Jacobite side. The Duke of Cumberland's forces included three battalions of Lowland Scots, a battalion of Highland Scots from Clan Munro, a large contingent of the Clan Campbell militia, and a fair number of foot soldiers from the clans of Grant, Gunn, MacKay, and Ross. The Bonnie Prince's army (which was three-quarters Highlanders with the rest made up of Lowlanders and French and Irish troops) was exhausted and starving and only a quarter of them even had swords! They fought bravely, but after little more than an hour of fighting, 1,250 of the Jacobites had been slain. The Hanoverian army lost just fifty-two men.

Did ye ken . . . ?

While he was on the run from the Hanoverians, one of the places where Bonnie Prince Charlie took refuge was Glenmoriston. An Edinburgh merchant called Roderick Mackenzie was traveling through Glenmoriston when he ran into a band of redcoats. Unfortunately for him, Mackenzie bore an uncanny resemblance to the errant prince, and the redcoats decided they had got their man. When Mackenzie refused to cooperate, they shot him. As he lay there dying, Mackenzie cried out, "Alas, you have killed your prince!" The redcoats promptly cut off his head and took it back to Fort Augustus, convinced that they had killed Bonnie Prince Charlie himself, when all they had really done was murder an innocent merchant. As a consequence, in Glenmoriston a cairn was raised in honor of the brave Roderick Mackenzie.

However, the Duke of Cumberland was hot on the heels of the retreating Scottish army and caught up with them at Culloden Moor on 16 April 1746. Ignoring the advice of Lord George Murray, his most experienced commander, Charles chose to fight on flat, open, and marshy ground, where his forces were exposed to the superior firepower of the British troops. To make matters worse, Charles found himself commanding his troops from a position from which he couldn't clearly see what was happening on the battlefield. Holding on to the vain hope that Cumberland's army would attack first, he left his men exposed to Hanoverian artillery for twenty minutes before finally ordering an attack. The ill-thought-out battle was an unmitigated disaster for the Jacobites, hence the line in the rhyme, "The lion beat the unicorn all around the town."

After their defeat at Culloden, Charlie and the other surviving Jacobites were forced to go on the run, having to rely on the charity and cover of their remaining supporters. These people helped as much as they could afford to—"Some gave them white bread and some gave them brown, some gave them plum cake"—but they risked their lives in doing so.

Determined to stamp out any further rebellion, the Duke of Cumberland's soldiers worked their way through the Highlands and islands of Scotland, killing, plundering and destroying houses and crops. In fact, his troops committed out so many atrocities in their relentless search for the fleeing rebels (having already executed all the prisoners and wounded on the battlefield after Culloden) that Prince William has been known to Scots as "The Butcher" ever since.

More than three thousand Jacobite sympathizers were arrested
of the 1745 Jacobite Rebellion. Most of them were imprisoned or t
colonies. However, one in twenty were picked for "show" executic
the rebellion, laws were passed to prevent Highlanders from carr
wearing their traditional tartan kilts. Bagpipes were banned, the clan ̩,
destroyed, and the Highland way of life never recovered.

Despite there being a reward of £30,000 for his capture, the Young Pretender
survived for five months on the run in Scotland. His flight from the Duke of Cumberland's redcoats has become the stuff of legend and is commemorated in "The Skye
Boat Song."

> Speed, bonnie boat, like a bird on the wing,
> Onward! the sailors cry;
> Carry the bairn that's born to be king,
> Over the sea to Skye.
>
> Loud the winds howl, loud the waves roar,
> Thunderclaps rend the air;
> Baffled, our foes stand by the shore;
> Follow, they will not dare.
>
> Though the waves leap, soft shall ye sleep,
> Ocean's a royal bed;
> Racked in the deep, Flora will keep
> Watch by your weary head.
>
> Many's the bairn fought on that day,
> Well the claymore could wield;
> When night came, silently lay
> Dead in Culloden's field.
>
> Burned are their homes, exile and death
> Scatter the loyal men;
> Yet e'er the sword cool in the sheath,
> Charlie will come again.

Incredibly, the song manages to make the dramatic, if somewhat humiliating,
story of the final stage of Charlie's escape from Scotland into a moving memorial. The
truth is that the Bonnie Prince was forced to disguise himself as a lady's maid and
pose as Betty Burke, maid to the twenty-four-year-old Flora MacDonald. Pity poor
Flora; for her part in the escape, she was later imprisoned in the Tower of London.

Many have assumed that "The Skye Boat Song" is a traditional Scottish tune
based on an ancient Gaelic rowing song. However, the lyrics were actually written in
1884 by Sir Harold Boulton (1859–1935), although the melody itself could indeed be
based on a traditional one. The song was just another aspect of the Victorian obses-

sion with the more picturesque moments in Scottish history as spearheaded by Sir Walter Scott.

After many adventures, assisted by his supporters, Bonnie Prince Charlie managed to evade capture and eventually escaped the country aboard a French frigate called *L'Heureux* (which translates, appropriately enough, as "The Fortunate One"). He was never to set foot on British soil again, returning to Rome where he was born, and where he lived the rest of his life in exile. Later in life, he was heard to say, "I should have died with my men at Culloden." So, in the end, the lion had won.

Did ye ken . . . ?

Modern Jacobites still believe that the true line of succession to the British throne runs through the Stuarts and their descendants, meaning that they consider Duke Franz of Bavaria should really by Francis II, King of England, Scotland, France, and Ireland. Duke Franz himself will not be drawn on the issue.

HOW DO YOU PLAY THE BAGPIPES?

Ask anyone what the national musical instrument of Scotland is, and they will tell you it's the bagpipes, but, curiously enough, they are not a Scottish invention. The bagpipes have been around a lot longer than Scotland has. It is likely that they were invented in Central Asia, and they are certainly ancient, possibly dating from as far back as 1,300 BC. For a start, they are mentioned in the Bible.

In the Old Testament book of Daniel, chapter 3, verse 5, it is written, "As soon as you hear the sound of the horn, flute, zither, lyre, harp, pipes and all kinds of music, you must fall down and worship the image of gold that King Nebuchadnezzar has set up." And then again in verse 10, "You have issued a decree, O king, that everyone who hears the sound of the horn, flute, zither, lyre, harp, pipes and all kinds of music must fall down and worship the image of gold . . ." And then in verse 15, "Now when you hear the sound of the horn, flute, zither, lyre, harp, pipes and all kinds of music . . ." Anyway, you get the idea.

Bagpipes (also known by pipers as simply "the pipes") also crop up in fourth-century Greek poetry, but the Romans probably brought them to Britain. The earliest Pictish carvings of a man playing a set of pipes don't appear until the eighth century AD.

Nero, the hated first-century AD Roman emperor, did not fiddle as Rome burned, as some will insist (the violin wasn't invented until the fifteenth century), but he was known to play the bagpipes. Dio Chrystostom, a Greek writing around AD 100, noted, "They say that he can write, carve statues, play the aulos both with his mouth, and also with the armpit, a bag being thrown under it."

Bagpipes are mentioned in Chaucer's *Canterbury Tales*, which were written around 1380: "A baggepype wel coude he blowe and sowne,/And ther-with-al he broghte us out of towne."

Bagpipes appear in Scottish literature around 1450, at a time when the use of bagpipes in southern England was dying out. By the middle of the sixteenth century, the Highland bagpipes were used as military instruments, announcing the call to arms, and for clan gatherings, specifically as a way of lamenting the dead. The continued

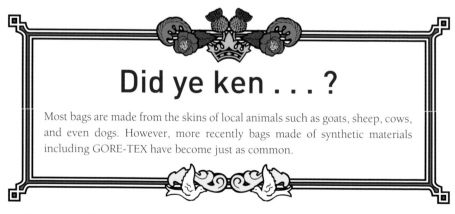

Did ye ken . . . ?

Most bags are made from the skins of local animals such as goats, sheep, cows, and even dogs. However, more recently bags made of synthetic materials including GORE-TEX have become just as common.

popularity and development of the Highland bagpipe could be put down to the special place that the piper held in Highland society. In later years, its use in the Scottish regiments of the British army would become just as important to its ongoing development as it was to the instrument's increasing its popularity around the world.

Bagpipes belong to a class of musical instrument known as *aerophones* that use enclosed reeds fed from a constant reservoir of air in the form of a bag. Although the Scottish Great Highland Bagpipe is the most well-known today, you will find bagpipes of many different kinds all over the world, from as places as far-flung as Northern Africa and the Persian Gulf to Scandinavia and Spain.

A set of bagpipes is made up of an air supply, a bag, a chanter, and a drone. There can be additional drones and even chanters in various combinations, held in place in stocks (the connectors with which the various pipes are attached to the bag).

The most common way of supplying air to the bag is by blowing into a blowpipe, or blowstick. A sixteenth- or seventeenth-century innovation that can be found in some pipes (such as the Irish uilleann pipes and the Northumbrian smallpipes) was to use a set of bellows to supply the air. The bag itself is an airtight reservoir that not only keeps the air contained but also regulates its flow, while the player breathes or pumps with a bellows. This allows the piper to maintain continuous sound for quite some time.

The chanter is the pipe that produces the melody; it is played using one or two hands. A chanter can be bored so that its inside walls are parallel for its full length, or it can be bored in the shape of a cone. The reed that is fitted into the chanter can be either a single or a double reed. The chanter is usually open-ended, meaning that there is no easy way for the piper to stop the pipe from making a noise once he or she has begun to play.

The drone is most commonly a cylindrical tube with a single reed, although drones with double reeds exist, and most bagpipes will have at least one. Depending on the type of pipes, the drones may lie over the shoulder (as with the Great Highland bagpipe), across the arm opposite the bag, or even parallel to the chanter. Native close-grained woods were once used to make the chanter and drone, but African blackwood is now the preferred material of choice among pipe makers.

Knowing the history of the bagpipes and knowing how the instrument is put together is one thing. Knowing how to play the bagpipes is another thing entirely, and mastery of the instruments takes years of practice.

Anyone who wants to learn to play the bagpipes starts off with a practice chanter, rather than a full set of pipes. A practice chanter looks like a simple flute or recorder with the addition of a double reed. Practice chanters were traditionally made of wood, but today plastic ones are more common, with half-size chanters available for the budding child piper.

The next stage involves moving on to the Highland bagpipe. This can be a big step, so the transition to full bagpipe is broken down to three basic stages: playing the bagpipe with the chanter "blocked off," playing the bagpipe with the drones blocked off, and playing the bagpipe with chanter and one or two drones blocked off. These stages are important in helping a new piper learn how to control the set, improve tuning, develop stamina, and develop a better ear. It's then simply a case of transferring the knowledge and technique gained using the practice chanter to the full pipes. Easy, eh?

Scottish music (or *ceòl*) is often presented at cèilidhs (*cèilidh* being the Gaelic for "concert") which feature forms of music as varied as the gentle music of the

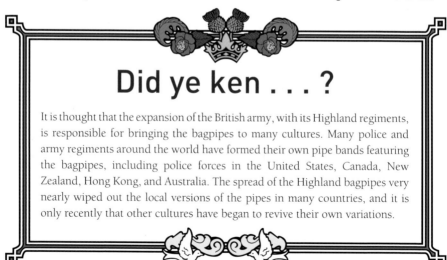

Did ye ken . . . ?

It is thought that the expansion of the British army, with its Highland regiments, is responsible for bringing the bagpipes to many cultures. Many police and army regiments around the world have formed their own pipe bands featuring the bagpipes, including police forces in the United States, Canada, New Zealand, Hong Kong, and Australia. The spread of the Highland bagpipes very nearly wiped out the local versions of the pipes in many countries, and it is only recently that other cultures have began to revive their own variations.

clàrsach (or "harp") and the robust sound of *pibroch* (from the Gaelic word *piobaireachd*, meaning "bagpipe music"). In the heyday of the clan, chiefs retained their own pipers and harpists. In the case of the Clan MacLeod of Dunvegan, Skye, their pipers came from several generations of one family, the MacCrimmons.

There are two kinds of bagpipe music (*ceòl na pìoba*): pibroch (*ceòl mòr*) and light music (*ceòl beag*). Both bagpipe and harp music have enjoyed increased popularity in recent times, with much more being done to promote both instruments. Pipers are often called upon to play at weddings, birthdays, funerals, various town events, and to "pipe in" the haggis on Burns'night. Other instruments that retain their popularity in the Highlands are the fiddle or violin (*an fhidheall*) and accordion (*am bocsa*).

However, such instruments were not so widespread in the Highlands in the past, and a form of singing was also used to accompany dancing. This is known as mouth music or *puirt-a-beul*, and unaccompanied singing is considered the most traditional form of Gaelic singing. One style of this unaccompanied singing is that of the waulking songs, which were used by groups of women working together to shrink tweed. Another distinctive form of Gaelic music is the psalm singing practiced in Gaelic services in Protestant churches. This involves a precentor giving out the line, as it is called, and the congregation then repeating the line with ornamentation.

Traditional Gaelic music also lives on in Scotland through the many festivals that are held throughout the country on an annual basis. The premier festival is the National Mod. Held annually in October, the Mod is a weeklong event. Much like the Welsh National Eisteddfod, it is a competitive festival. There are major awards for solo and choral singing, but piping, the sport of shinty, and drama also feature prominently. Local Mods are held throughout Scotland in May and June.

WHAT ARE THE SCOTTISH HIGHLANDS?

Most of those things that one thinks of when they think of Scotland—the clans, tartan, bagpipes, heather, porridge, and whisky—are things that you would find in the Scottish Highlands, the mountainous region at the far northern end of the British Isles. The imaginary Highland Line, which divides the Highlands from the Lowlands, has been drawn in various places in the past but is now generally accepted to run between the Moray Firth (on the east coast) to the Clyde estuary (on the west). Everything that lies west and north of this line is taken to be the Highlands.

The Highlands of Scotland are Britain's last great wilderness—as ruggedly beautiful as they are barren—and contain some of the country's most dramatic scenery. The Great Glen is an impressive valley more than sixty miles long that divides Scotland diagonally between northwest and southeast. Ben Nevis, the highest peak in Scotland (and, indeed, the British Isles) at 4,909 feet (1,344 meters), looms over the southern end. Between 1803 and 1847, the Caledonian Canal was cut to link the four lochs that lie in the Glen, making it possible for boats to sail from the Irish Sea to the North Sea.

The Highlands are also where you will find the Scottish Munros. There are 284 Munros in Scotland, or, to put it another way, mountains that are over 3,000 feet (915 meters) in height. This list of Scottish peaks was first drawn up by Sir Hugh Munro and published in 1891. It has been revised over the years, with the most recent version being produced in 1997. The smallest peaks, all measuring 3,000 feet (915 meters) are Ben Vane, Sgurr nan Ceannaichean and Beinn Teallach, while the tallest three are Braeriach at 4,252 feet (1,296 meters), Ben Macdui at 4,295 feet (1,309 meters) and, at the top of the list, Ben Nevis.

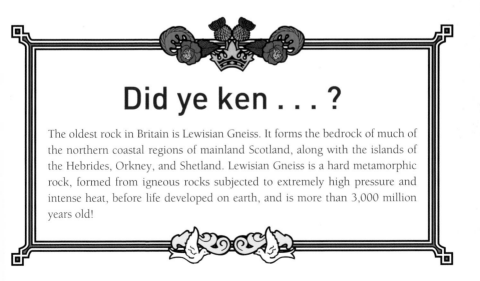

Did ye ken . . . ?

The oldest rock in Britain is Lewisian Gneiss. It forms the bedrock of much of the northern coastal regions of mainland Scotland, along with the islands of the Hebrides, Orkney, and Shetland. Lewisian Gneiss is a hard metamorphic rock, formed from igneous rocks subjected to extremely high pressure and intense heat, before life developed on earth, and is more than 3,000 million years old!

You will find the greatest wealth of Scottish wildlife in the wilds of the Highlands and the islands, and some of the animals that live there are rarely found living wild anywhere else in the British Isles. You are unlikely to find red deer outside the Scottish Highlands. The golden eagle, one of the country's most enduring emblems, is found soaring over the mountain peaks there. Shetland ponies, with their thick, wiry coats and reduced stature, are indigenous to the cold, windswept, northerly Shetland Isles. Highland cattle have been bred in Scotland since the sixteenth century and are instantly recognizable due to their thick shaggy coats and long, gently curving horns.

On Scotland's coasts you will find puffins, guillemots, kittiwakes, and gannets, and the coastal waters are also home to gray seals, whales, and dolphins. The country's sea lochs, freshwater lochs, and rivers sustain a myriad of animal and insect species, including wild salmon, trout, otters, and dragonflies. In the hills and mountains, you will find rare arctic and alpine plants. Sheep graze on grass and heather, and birds of prey such as the kestrel scour the bleak moorland terrain for mice and voles. Some of Scotland's ancient forests are now protected and provide a woodland refuge for red squirrels, goldcrests, pine martens, and wildcats.

Did ye ken . . . ?

In 1773, the Scottish writer and biographer James Boswell helped launch the tourist industry in Scotland when he persuaded his English friend, Dr. Samuel Johnson (author of the first English dictionary), to take an extensive tour of the Highlands and wrote a popular book about it called *Journal of a Tour to the Hebrides.*

For the people who live and work in the Highlands of Scotland, crofting and fishing have been the traditional mainstays of the West Highland and island economy. Crofting is a form of agriculture based on a unit of land known as a croft. Worked by crofters, the crofts themselves vary in size from very small units of land to large areas, comparable to the smaller farms of the central and eastern Highlands. However, few crofters can earn a living from agriculture these days, and most have other jobs to sustain them, working their crofts on only a part-time basis. The fishing industry in Scotland has shrunk in recent years as well, so fewer crofters now combine the harvest of the land with the harvest of the ocean.

Other traditional industries in the Highlands and islands, however, continue to offer significant employment. These include the production of Harris Tweed and whisky distilling. Despite being prone to fluctuating levels of demand, Harris Tweed remains a major employer in Lewis and Harris, where the cloth is woven in the homes of weavers before being finished in the mills of Stornoway. Whisky is produced by distilleries throughout the Highlands, but the island of Islay (renowned for its distinctive malts) claims the greatest concentration of production, having, as it does, seven distilleries!

Of course, in the age of the automobile, Highlanders are also employed in the oil industry either offshore on the oil rigs or in the platform construction yards. Tourism is now the major growth industry in the Highlands, even though it is largely seasonal and subject to the notorious Scottish climate. Despite not enjoying the best weather the U.K. has to offer, the scenic beauty of the Highlands still attracts large numbers of tourists each year.

The tourist season has been extended in some areas thanks to the development of winter ski facilities. The main skiing centers are Glenshee, the Cairngorms, the Lecht, Glencoe, and Aonach Mor. These areas are also popular with hill-walkers and climbers, as are Torridon and the Cuillins. Anglers visit the rivers Spey, Tay, and Tweed to fish for salmon and trout, while other water sports (such as sailing) are

Did ye ken . . . ?

In 1820, the events at the Invergarry Games included "dancing, piping, lifting a heavy stone, throwing the hammer and running from the island to Invergarry and back" and "twisting the legs of a cow." The person who could twist all four legs off a dead cow the quickest was declared the winner!

especially popular on Loch Lomond, Loch Tay, and Loch Morlich, as well as in the Firth of Clyde itself.

Of course, the tourists also come to Scotland to enjoy the traditional Highland Games. More than seventy Highland Games meetings are now held in the country each year, but the most famous take place at Braemar in Aberdeenshire, in September, and are attended by the royal family.

The Highland Games were traditionally organized by clan chiefs to find the strongest men to be bodyguards, the fastest to act as couriers, and the fittest to fight in their armies. The best pipers and dancers were also hired to be their personal entertainers. Events include tug-of-war, the shot put, throwing the hammer, Highland dancing, running, jumping, the pole vault, and tossing the caber, which is a pole 20 feet (6 meters) long, weighing more than 110 pounds (50 kilograms).

Historically, the Scottish Highlands are also remembered for the Highland Clearances, when thousands of Gaelic-speaking Scots from the Highlands and islands were evicted by landlords. In many cases the landlords were the very men who would have been their own clan chiefs. From around 1760, and well into Queen Victoria's reign, landowners systematically turned people off the land they had farmed for hundreds of years and replaced them with sheep, cattle and, later, deer forests. This process of mass eviction became known as the "Highland Clearances." Many of the landowners, much more interested in maximizing the profit from their vast Highland estates, no longer felt a sense of responsibility toward the people who scraped out a living on their land.

Some of those evicted in this way joined up with the Scottish regiments that fought in the Napoleonic Wars. Thousands more left Scotland altogether, with many Highlanders emigrating to North America, as well as one of Britain's newest colonies—Australia. The Allan Line was one of the many companies that promised to transport desperate Highlanders across the seas and to a new life in "all parts of Canada and the United States." When they reached the New World, some found work on farms and plantations, but life was very hard, and many of the new immigrants suffered badly.

Did ye ken . . . ?

In 1845, eighteen families were thrown out of their houses in Glencalvie, Ross-shire. Their only place of refuge was the churchyard at Croick, where they attempted to shelter under a makeshift tent. Before they finally left to move to a town, or to emigrate, some scratched their names and messages on the windows of the church. The scratches are still there today.

WHY IS TARTAN SO
IMPORTANT TO THE SCOTS?

Tartan is a pattern consisting of crisscross horizontal and vertical bands in multiple colors, but the word "tartan" has also come to mean the cloth bearing this pattern, which was used in traditional Highland dress. It is still used to make kilts as well as to decorate boxes of shortbread and the like. Why have tartans become synonymous with Scotland, Scottish clans, and particular Scottish families?

The word "tartan" comes from the French *tiretain* (which denoted a type of material—nothing more) and originally described the way the thread was woven to make the cloth. In tartan cloth, each thread passes over two threads, then under two threads, and so on, forming the visible diagonal lines where different colors cross, which, in turn, give the appearance of new colors blended from the original ones. A tartan pattern is unlike a check because in a tartan there is always a square where the two colors of thread cross, forming a speckled blend of the two.

The process of actually making tartan begins with the gathering of the wool, the fibers of which, having been suitably prepared, are then spun into yarn. The woollen yarn thus produced is then dyed, using natural plant dyes. Having woven the thread into tartan cloth, the final stage of the process is to waulk the cloth, whereby the wool is turned into felt.

Tartan has been worn by the Scots since at least the thirteenth century, and the oldest known piece of tartan was found in a pot filled with over 1,900 silver Roman coins, buried in the ground near Falkirk and thought to be 1,700 years old. This Falkirk tartan, as it is known, is a simple check design, of natural light and dark wool.

However, tartan itself is even older than that. The Hallstatt culture of Central Europe, which flourished between 400 BC and 100 BC, produced tartanlike textiles. Some were recently discovered in Salzburg, Austria, and tartanlike leggings were found on the Cherchen Man, a three thousand-year-old mummy uncovered in the Taklamakan Desert in western China. Similar discoveries have been made in central Europe and Scandinavia.

Did ye ken . . . ?

Although tartan is also known as plaid in North America, in Scotland, a "plaid" is specifically a tartan cloth slung over the shoulder, and comes from the Scottish Gaelic *plaide*, meaning "blanket."

Did ye ken . . . ?

The earliest image of Scottish soldiers wearing tartan is a woodcut dating from 1631. After the failed Jacobite Rebellion of 1745, the government attempted to bring the warrior clans under control by banning tartan and other aspects of Gaelic culture, via the Dress Act of 1746. The Black Watch pattern (also known as Campbell, Grant Hunting, Universal, or Government) was the only tartan allowed by law. This pattern was used by the regiments raised within Scotland in 1729 (to keep peace in the Highlands), and formed the basis of the regimental tartans still in use today. In fact, many tartans in use today are based on the three-color design of Black Watch.

In Highland Scotland, there was a different pattern of stripes for each distinct district or clan, and it was worn as a single length of tartan plaid draped over the shoulder and held at the waist with a belt.

Even as late as the 1830s tartan was sometimes described as being, "plain coloured . . . without pattern." The patterned cloth made in the Scottish Highlands was actually called *breacan*, a Gaelic word meaning "many colors." In time tartan and *breacan* combined to describe a certain type of pattern on a certain type of cloth. The pattern of a tartan is called a *sett*, which is made up of a series of woven threads that cross at right angles.

Tartans were originally a style of cloth intended only to be decorative. They were made from local wool using only a limited range of color dye. They featured patterns popular within the districts where they were manufactured. It is because of this that certain tartans have become so inextricably connected with particular regions and clans.

Until the middle of the nineteenth century, the Highland tartans were associated only with specific regions or districts. Where there was a strong clan within a district, as was often the case in the Highlands, visitors from other areas would have been recognized as being from a different clan because their tartan was different. Thus, the idea of the clan tartans was born.

In the early nineteenth century, people started to realize that the knowledge of tartans was being lost. At the same time there was a romantic movement concerning Scotland's past, which led to institutional, as well as individual, efforts to preserve specific tartan designs. Some cultural historians, however, hold that the elaborate system of clan tartans was purely an invention of this time and had not existed before at all. Whatever the truth of the matter, in the early 1800s people set about reconstructing tartans from portraits, collected them on pilgrimages, recovered designs from original weaver's notes, and even demanded them from clan chiefs.

William Wilson & Sons, of Bannockburn, became suppliers of tartan to the military around the year 1770. Wilson corresponded with his agents in the Highlands, gaining information and samples of cloth from the clan districts, which then enabled him to reproduce "perfectly genuine patterns." He recorded over two hundred *setts* by 1822, many of which were simply given a number or, in some cases, fanciful names such as "the Robin Hood tartan."

This tartan renaissance was boosted by the visit to Edinburgh of George IV in 1822, with Sir Walter Scott urging his fellow countrymen to attend, "all plaided and plumed in their tartan array." The king was met by chieftains and clansmen in new tartan and was cheered as "the chief of the chiefs." The festivities surrounding the event (George was the first reigning monarch to visit Scotland in 171 years) brought a sudden demand for tartan cloth and made it the national dress of the whole of Scotland rather than just the Highlands and islands. Following the royal visit, several books that documented tartans (including James Logan's romanticized work *The Scottish Gael,* published in 1831), added to the craze.

The first publication that included plates of clan tartans was the *Vestiarium Scoticum* published in 1842, and the work of two brothers, John Sobieski and Charles Allen Hay. The brothers actually called themselves John Sobieski Stolberg Stuart and Charles Edward Stuart. They first appeared in Scotland in 1822, claiming to be grandsons of Prince Charles Edward Stuart (a.k.a. Bonnie Prince Charlie) and his wife Princess Louise of Stolberg. These Sobieski Stuarts also claimed that the *Vestiarium* was based on a copy of an existing ancient manuscript on clan tartans. However, they were never able to produce the mysterious document.

Queen Victoria also gave considerable encouragement to the tartan revival, going on to design her own tartan (called, appropriately enough, the Victoria). Prince Albert designed the Balmoral tartan that is still used as a royal tartan today. The distinctive Royal Stewart Tartan is the personal tartan of Victoria's great-great-granddaughter, Her Majesty Queen Elizabeth II.

Did ye ken . . . ?

Bizarrely, the oldest recognized tartan design is actually shared with England, Scotland's ancient rival. It is a tasteful black-and-white check known as the Northumbria or Border tartan.

Did ye ken . . . ?

Contrary to popular belief, there is no law proclaiming who can or can't wear a particular tartan. If there is any control at all, it is only governed by convention. However, disputes relating to the use of a particular pattern can be tried under the civil law of the Copyright, Designs and Patents Act and in rare cases by trademark. For example, the Burberry Check (first designed in early 1920s) is patented and protected by trademark.

According to the Scottish Tartans Authority, the Balmoral tartan should only be worn by members of the British royal family. However, this doesn't stop some weavers outside the U.K. from ignoring the long-standing convention of the Royal Family's right to this tartan. The best deterrent the society can offer nonroyals who wear the Balmoral is that they will be treated with great disdain by the Scottish tartan industry.

The significance of tartan as national dress led to the creation of clan tartans for every Scottish family name, including those that previously had none. There were also hunting tartans, of a more subdued character, and brighter dress tartans. Tartans changed according to fashion and trade tartans began to fill any and every

Did ye ken . . . ?

In recent years corporate tartans have become popular, whereby an institution or company adopts a tartan design for its livery and to use in merchandising. You can even have tartans now in a variety of color effects, called Modern, Ancient, and Muted. Modern represents a tartan that is colored using chemical dye rather than natural dye. Ancient refers to a lighter shade of tartan, supposed to represent the colors that would be obtained by using natural dyes. Muted (or Reproduction) refers to tartan in shades between modern and ancient and dates from the early 1970s but is said to be the closest match to the shades achieved using natural dyes before the mid-nineteenth century.

Did ye ken . . . ?

The world's first color photograph was made by the Scottish scientist James Clerk Maxwell in 1861 and featured a tartan ribbon.

niche available, from dancing tartans to mourning tartans (designed using combinations of black and white).

Today's dress tartans are based on the *earasaid* tartans worn by Highland women in the seventeenth and eighteenth centuries, and tend to be made by replacing a prominent color with white. Their most common use today is in Highland dancing. In Scotland today, there are also at least two local government councils with official tartans.

As well as creating new tartans, Victorian entrepreneurs were also responsible for producing new tartan objects called "tartanware." They are still widely collected throughout England and Scotland today. The distinctive cloth patterns were incorporated into everything from snuffboxes and jewelery cases to tableware and sewing accessories. Some of the more popular tartans for this use were the Stewart, McDonald, McGregor, McDuff, MacBeth, and Prince Charlie.

A tartan pattern is formed from a single list of colored threads called a thread count. Every tartan consists of an under check (formed of the broader bands of color) and the over check (the narrower lines of color that are used to decorate or embellish it). It is possible to "read" a tartan, in order to tell which clan or region it comes from, but to acquire this skill requires practice and the ability to find two unique points within the pattern called the pivots.

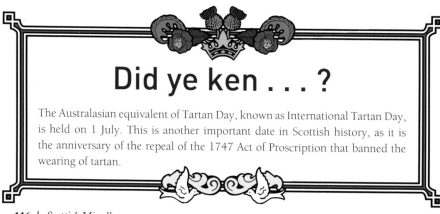

Did ye ken . . . ?

The Australasian equivalent of Tartan Day, known as International Tartan Day, is held on 1 July. This is another important date in Scottish history, as it is the anniversary of the repeal of the 1747 Act of Proscription that banned the wearing of tartan.

It has been estimated that there are about seven thousand different tartans, with another 150 new designs being created every year. The Scottish Register of Tartans is Scotland's official tartan register, and is maintained and administrated by the National Archives of Scotland, based in Edinburgh. On the Register's Web site users can register new tartan designs, search for and request the thread counts of existing tartans, and even receive notifications of newly registered tartans.

The idea that the various colors used in tartan had specific meanings is another modern invention. One such myth is that red tartans were "battle tartans," colored so they would not show blood. However, many more recently created tartans, such as Canadian provincial and territorial tartans as well as American state tartans, are designed with certain symbolic meanings in mind. For example the color green can symbolize prairies or forests, blue represents lakes and rivers, and yellow is sometimes used to symbolize certain crops.

Tartan Day is held on 6 April in Canada and the United States as a celebration of Scottish heritage recognizing the influence Scottish immigrants have had on these two countries in particular. Why 6 April? Because that was the date on which the Declaration of Arbroath (effectively Scotland's Declaration of Independence) was signed in 1320. Tartan Day began as a one-off event, held in New York City in 1982, but the current format originated in Canada in 1986, when it was proposed at a meeting of the Federation of Scottish Clans in Nova Scotia. It spread to other Scots communities in other countries during the 1990s, but wasn't officially celebrated in Scotland until 2004, although the Scottish tourist board now exploits the festivities to promote tourism in Scotland itself. Tartan Day celebrations generally include parades of pipe bands, Highland dancing, and other suitably Scottish-themed events.

WHAT DOES A SCOTSMAN
WEAR UNDER HIS KILT, AND
WHAT DOES HE KEEP IN HIS
SPORRAN?

"A man in a kilt is a man and a half," or so the expression would have it. Once the daily dress of Scottish clansmen, the kilt is now largely reserved for more formal or even ceremonial occasions, and is instantly recognizable as being part of the national dress of Scotland. Or as Ambrose Bierce would put it in *The Devil's Dictionary*, a kilt is, "a costume sometimes worn by Scotchmen in America and Americans in Scotland."

Like so much else that we think of today as being quintessentially Scottish, the kilt did not actually originate in Scotland at all. As we have already seen, the Scoti tribe emigrated from Ireland around in the fourth century AD, displacing the native Pictish people and bringing with them the Irish dress of their homeland. This was made up of a *léine* and a *brat*. The *léine* was rather like a linen (or sometimes silk) undertunic, white (or at least unbleached), decorated with red or gold embroidery, and sometimes hooded. Women wore it long, but a man's *léine* ended at his knees.

The earliest authentic mention of a kilt appears in the Norse history of Magnus Barefoot. Written around 1097, it relates that upon returning from his conquest of the Hebrides, Magnus adopted the dress that was popular among the islanders there. As a consequence he went about bare-legged, wearing a short tunic. A fifteenth-century historian remarked that the Highland gentlemen of his day, "wore no covering from the middle of the thigh to the foot, clothing themselves with a mantle instead of an upper garment, and a shirt dyed with saffron." Other depictions of the *léine* show it only reaching to mid-thigh, like a short kilt. However, it was never made of wool or plaid material.

By the Elizabethan age, this fashionable item had become a full-pleated smock made from at least seven yards of fabric! It was always made of linen and it was usually yellow. The English referred to it as the "saffron shirt." In 1537 Henry VIII banned its use in Ireland, because saffron was a very expensive natural dye. Even today, top-grade Spanish *mancha* saffron costs around $5,680 per pound, but then it does take between 85,000 and 140,000 crocuses to make just 2 pounds (1 kilogram) of the stuff! As a result, the bright yellow dye it produced was a luxury reserved for the nobility—and was certainly not for the common Irish, as far as King Henry was concerned!

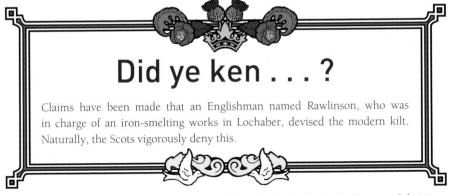

Did ye ken . . . ?

Claims have been made that an Englishman named Rawlinson, who was in charge of an iron-smelting works in Lochaber, devised the modern kilt. Naturally, the Scots vigorously deny this.

The *brat* is a rectangular piece of cloth thrown around the body and fastened on the breast or shoulder by a brooch. Both men and women wore them, and the advantage of the *brat* was that it could be wrapped around the shoulders or looped under the sword arm for better manoeuvrability. *Brats* could be worn in varying lengths, depending on the occasion or the rank of the wearer. Some tales speak of the queen's *brat* dragging on the ground behind her chariot. They were also worn in many colors, which was another sign of nobility.

The sporran, held by a chain strap, sits at the center of the front apron of the kilt and is supposed to be worn with it. The sporran (which is Gaelic for "purse") ranges in style and material (usually leather or fur), and performs the same function as pockets do in a pair of trousers.

Curiously, the origin of the word "kilt" is neither Scots nor Gaelic. The word was first used in the eighteenth century and some believe it comes from the English "quilt," either because the padding of the kilt's pleats produce a quilted effect or because the kilt, in its original plaid form, was a bedcover. Others say that the word "kilt" derives from the Danish *kilte op*, meaning "tuck up."

Nowadays, when people talk of kilts, what they are really referring to is the great kilt, or plaid. This is the traditional Scottish garment passed down from the Irish Scoti tribe, made from three to six yards' worth of full-width fabric. In the 1500s to 1700, when the great kilt was worn, it would not have been made from tartan. Instead, great kilts were made from naturally dyed wool and, as a result, the colors would have been noticeably muted compared to what we're used to today.

If you've ever wondered how to go about folding a kilt correctly, here's a fairly simple ten-step method:

1. Begin by putting on the shirt and waistcoat you want to wear with the great kilt. You will need to make sure you have a belt at hand as well.
2. Estimate your body width using the span of your hands as a convenient measure.
3. Laying out the kilt fabric lengthways on the floor, use the measurement you took of your waist to measure out the width of your body on the fabric.
4. Gather the fabric together to form three sections. The first and third sections should be slightly wider than the measurement you took of your body.
5. Neatly pleat the wider middle section of fabric until it is roughly the same width as the other two.
6. Take the belt and push it underneath the material.
7. Lie down on top of the folded fabric with your waist at the same level as the belt. The hem of the kilt should just reach the middle of your knees.
8. Wrap the right side of the garment over yourself. When this is lying neatly, fasten the belt. Once you are happy that the hem is straight and level, be bold and stand up.
9. Taking the center of the plaid in both hands, draw it backward, tucking the central section into the belt on both sides.

10. Holding both ends of the plaid in your left hand, draw them over your left shoulder and fasten the material to your shirt, or waistcoat, with a suitable plaid brooch. And, och aye the noo, you'll look like a Scotsman! What should you wear under your kilt? The answer—nothing!

Did ye ken . . . ?

Christmas 1644 brought a most unpleasant "gift" to Scotland—the plague, brought by ship from Europe via the port of Leith. It first took hold in Edinburgh before spreading north and west. Over the next eighteen months, the "pest" (as some called it) killed a substantial part of the Scottish population. In an effort to halt the spread of the plague, certain everyday activities were banned, including wakes, penny weddings, and the wearing of the plaid—in other words, kilts! The reason for this was that people could hide signs of the sickness under the garment, which was not only worn kilted around the body but also often over the head.

What does a Scotsman wear under his kilt, and what does he keep in his sporran?

WHAT DOES A HAMBURGER GIANT HAVE TO DO WITH THE SCOTTISH CLANS?

The name McDonald's and the golden arches logo are famous the word over. How did the name of one of Scotland's most famous clans become synonymous with hamburgers, fast food, and a disconcertingly cheerful clown?

The McDonald's Corporation is the world's largest hamburger restaurant chain, its fast food outlets serving nearly forty-seven million customers every day. McDonald's mainly sells hamburgers, cheeseburgers, chicken products, french fries, breakfast items, soft drinks, milkshakes, and desserts. In recent years, the company has also expanded its menu to include alternative meal options, particularly salads, fruit, and snack wraps, in order to capitalize on growing consumer interest in health and wellness as well as in response to criticism over the healthfulness of its products and growing trends in obesity in Western nations.

The company was founded in 1940, when brothers Dick and Mac McDonald opened a restaurant in San Bernardino, California. However, this was not their first venture into fast food. In 1927 they opened a hamburger stand called "The Airdrome" at Monrovia airport in California. In 1948, having noticed that almost all of their profits came from hamburgers, they introduced the "Speedee Service System," thereby establishing the principles of the modern fast-food restaurant. At the time, their burgers cost fifteen cents, which was half as expensive as those at standard diners, but most importantly, theirs were served immediately. The restaurant was extremely successful, and its fame soon spread by word of mouth.

However, the present corporation dates its founding to the opening of a franchised restaurant in Des Plaines, Illinois, by Ray Kroc on 15 April 1955. This was actually the ninth McDonald's restaurant. Kroc, an entrepreneur and milkshake-mixer salesman, later purchased the McDonald brothers' share in the company.

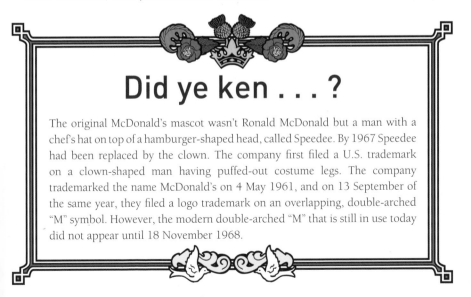

Did ye ken . . . ?

The original McDonald's mascot wasn't Ronald McDonald but a man with a chef's hat on top of a hamburger-shaped head, called Speedee. By 1967 Speedee had been replaced by the clown. The company first filed a U.S. trademark on a clown-shaped man having puffed-out costume legs. The company trademarked the name McDonald's on 4 May 1961, and on 13 September of the same year, they filed a logo trademark on an overlapping, double-arched "M" symbol. However, the modern double-arched "M" that is still in use today did not appear until 18 November 1968.

Did ye ken . . . ?

Portugal is the only country where McDonald's restaurants serve soup. This deviation from the standard menu depending on local tastes is a characteristic for which the chain is well known. It means that the company abides by regional food taboos—such as the religious prohibition on eating beef in India—and is able to make available foods with which the regional market is more familiar, such as the sale of McRice in Indonesia.

Kroc's ambition led to its the company's worldwide expansion. The company was listed on the public stock markets in 1965.

Roy Kroc—later nicknamed "The Big M"— was known for his aggressive business practices, which eventually forced the McDonald brothers to leave the fast-food industry altogether, having feuded over control of the business for a number of years. The site of the McDonald brothers' original restaurant in San Bernardino is now a monument.

The first McDonald's restaurants opened in the United States, Canada, Costa Rica, Panama, Japan, the Netherlands, Germany, Australia, France, El Salvador, and Sweden. In 1958, McDonald's sold its 100 millionth hamburger worldwide, and a year later, in 1959, the 100th McDonald's restaurant opened in Fond du Lac, Wisconsin. In 1963 the company sold its one billionth hamburger and, in Toledo, Ohio, opened its 500th restaurant. On 12 October 1974, the first McDonald's in the U.K. opened in

Did ye ken . . . ?

There are a number of McDonald's restaurants with special themes. These include the "Solid Gold McDonald's" in Milwaukee, Wisconsin, which is a 1950s rock-and-roll-style outlet. In Victoria, British Columbia, there is even a McDonald's with a 24-carat-gold chandelier and associated light fixtures!

Did ye ken . . . ?

After Charles II died, his unpopular brother James II (James VII of Scotland), a Catholic, was driven into exile in France. The English replaced him with his own daughter Mary and her husband, William of Orange. The new king was persuaded to offer peace terms to the Highland clans if they would swear allegiance to him. When the leader of the MacDonalds of Glencoe missed the deadline for the oath of allegiance, William decided to make an example of him. He ordered the tragic massacre of the MacDonald clan in Glencoe—an act of violence that lives on to this day in Scottish memory.

Woolwich, southeast London. Overall, it was the company's 3,000th restaurant. It is estimated that McDonald's has now sold more than 100 billion hamburgers at more than 31,000 restaurants worldwide, employing more than one-and-a-half million people in 119 different countries and territories. *The Economist* magazine uses the "Big Mac Index" (which compares the cost of a Big Mac in various world currencies) to informally judge these currencies' purchasing power parity. Scandinavian countries lead the Big Mac Index, claiming four of the five most expensive Big Macs.

McDonald's the fast-food franchise is connected to the MacDonald clan of Scotland in name only. The clan system was the way by which Highland society was divided into tribal groups led by autocratic chiefs, and can be traced back as far as the twelfth century. All members of a clan bore the name of their chief even though they were not all actually blood relatives. The clansmen followed noble codes of hospitality, but first and foremost they were warriors.

The clan chief was its patriarch; he served as the clan's judge as well as its leader in battle. He commanded absolute loyalty from his clansmen, who, in return for his protection, gave him military service. When the time came to do battle with the enemy, the clan chief would summon his clan to him by sending a runner across his lands, bearing a burning cross! Below the clan chief were the chieftains of the septs (sub-units of the clan), and after them came the tacksmen, major tenants of the chief who were often related to him personally. The tacksmen sublet their land to other tenants, who formed the bottom strata of the social scale. Of course, after the Battle of Culloden, as we have already learned, all clan lands became forfeit and were seized by the crown.

Up until the ill-fated Jacobite Rebellion of 1745, the MacDonalds were the most powerful of all the clans and held the title Lords of the Isles. Every clan has

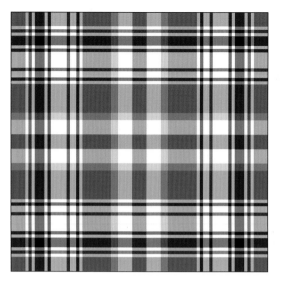

a plant badge, because in centuries past, the warriors of a particular clan would all wear a sprig of the same plant or tree in order to identify themselves in battle. In the case of the MacDonalds, this plant badge is heather. The clan crest (a heraldic device officially recognized by the Lord Lyon King of Arms and the personal property of the chief of the clan) is an armored hand holding a cross, and the clan's motto is *Per Mare Per Terras* (meaning, "By Sea and By Land"). It was not until the late seventeenth century that certain tartans became more closely associated with particular clans, but the MacDonald tartan is now instantly recognizable due to its broad bands of white and black and thin line of red detailing.

Although the Scottish clans exist nowadays in name only, they are still a strong source of pride for the Scots. Many still live in areas associated with their ancestral clans and many are those, both in Scotland and abroad, who can trace their roots back to the Highlands.

Did ye ken . . . ?

Haggis is nicknamed "The Great Chieftain o' the Puddin' Race," the title coming from the poem "Address to a Haggis" by Robert Burns, Scotland's national poet.

HOW DO YOU MAKE A
HAGGIS?

A longside the tartan kilt and the bagpipes, haggis has to be one of the most recognized symbols of Scotland and is undoubtedly its most famous dish. When I was a child, my father told me that you could see wild haggis running free in the Highlands of Scotland. He also said that the legs on one side of their bodies were shorter than those on the other because they spent all their days running around the steep peaks of Scottish mountains.

Now, before we go any further, let's get one thing straight—a haggis is not a real wee beastie. But it is the quintessential Scottish dish, made from some of the less choice-sounding cuts of mutton. However, the haggis actually started out as an ancient Greek sausage. The playwright Aristophanes refers to one exploding in his masterwork of 423 BC *The Clouds.* It was also a popular dish in England until the eighteenth century.

There is some dispute over the origin of the word "haggis." Some say it comes from the French for mince (*hachis*) while others hold that it comes from the Scots *hag,* meaning "to chop" or "hack." A commonly upheld myth regarding the recipe for haggis is that it was given to the Scots by the French at the time of the Auld Alliance. However, it is more likely that Scotland gave the haggis recipe to France. During the Middle Ages in France, haggis was called *le pain bénite de l, Ecosse*—literally, "the holy bread of Scotland."

They say, "Haggis is a braw dish, so long as ye dinnae look at the ingredients!" The dish was traditionally made out of cheap or leftover ingredients to make a tasty, filling meal, including a sheep's stomach, lungs, liver, heart, and tongue, along with beef suet, oatmeal, onions, pepper, and salt.

The first haggis recipe was printed in the 1787 edition of a cookery book by Mrs. McIver, and another appeared in *The Cook and Housewife's Manual,* published in 1826. In 2007, Lindsay Grieve, a traditional Scottish family butcher based in Hawick, estimated that he alone made more than 160,000 handmade haggis every year!

For the last twenty-one years, all haggises imported into the United States have been missing one vital ingredient, and the estimated six million Americans of Scottish descent have had to celebrate Burns' Night without an authentic haggis. And it's all down to the fact that Scotland's national dish is made with minced sheep's offal.

During the mad cow disease crisis, in 1989 the U.S. authorities banned haggis from being imported into the country, fearing that its constituent ingredients could be hazardous to health if consumed. Since that time, American butchers have attempted to make their own versions of haggis, all of which have ultimately been unsuccessful due to the fact that they were missing the very thing that makes a traditional haggis a haggis in the first place! Some U.S. versions are even made from beef, which means that most Scottish Americans don't actually know what a genuine haggis tastes like.

However, at the time of writing, the United States Department of Agriculture is considering lifting the long-standing import ban on haggis, following a ruling from the World Organization for Animal Health stating that sheep's lung is safe to eat. That means that come next Burns' Night, you could be enjoying an authentic haggis from Scotland, made with sheep's heart, liver, lung, and all.

If you like the idea of making your own haggis, here's the traditional method of making one:

Traditional Scottish Haggis

The bag of 1 sheep's stomach
1 sheep's pluck (the animal's liver, lungs, and heart)
9 oz. (250 g) beef suet
5 oz. (150 g) oatmeal
3 onions
salt and black pepper
a pinch of cayenne pepper
¼ pint (150 mls) of stock or gravy

Clean out the sheep's stomach thoroughly and leave it to soak overnight. In the morning turn it inside out. Wash the pluck and boil for 1½ hours, making sure that the windpipe (which will still be attached to the lungs) hangs over the edge of the pot to allow the impurities to drain from it. Mince the heart and lungs and grate half the liver into the mix. Chop the onions and suet together. While you are doing this, warm the oatmeal in the oven.

When all of the above ingredients are ready, mix them together, seasoning with the salt and pepper. Last of all add the cayenne for a spicy kick. Pour in some of the water that the pluck was boiled in over the mixture to give it a watery consistency. Half fill the stomach bag with the mixture, press out the air, and sew up the bag. Boil the haggis in a pan, with the lid left off, for 3 hours, but be on hand to prick the bag with a needle if it looks like it's going to burst. Serve with neeps and tatties. "Neeps" is mashed-up turnip or rutabaga, usually with a bit of milk (or lots of butter), and "tatties" are potatoes.

If that all sounds a little bit too much like hard work, then why not try this simplified version instead?

Easy Haggis

2 lamb kidneys
12 oz. (350 g) lamb shoulder
4½ oz. (125 g) beef suet
9 oz. (250 g) beef liver
1 cup of oatmeal
1 cup of stock
2 pureed onions
salt and pepper

Did ye ken . . . ?

A popular chip-shop dish throughout Scotland is the haggis supper, which is a long haggis pudding, shaped like a sausage, served with french fries. Some chippers (as chip shops are known by Scottish people) serve the traditional large round haggis puddings, though these tend to be too large for most appetites and some find them too spicy.

Boil the meat for about an hour and allow to cool. Chop the meaty ingredients into small pieces and grate the liver. Toast the oatmeal in the oven in a shallow dish, shaking occasionally. When all of the ingredients have been prepared, mix them together before spooning into a well-greased glass bowl. Cover with several layers of foil, and steam in a pan of boiling water for two hours. When ready, serve piping hot with neeps and tatties.

The perfect haggis should not be too moist or too dry and should be slightly spicy. The correct way to eat the dish is to take a bit of the haggis, neeps, and tatties on your fork at a time. Of course it's even better if it's washed down with a wee dram of whisky, and some people like to add some whisky to the haggis before cooking it!

Other haggis recipes include haggis lasagna, haggis rolls, haggis in pita with tzatsiki, haggis toasties, haggis pie, haggis hash brown, venison haggis, Indian haggis (made using traditional Indian spices), and haggis pizza. It is now possible to buy tinned haggis and haggis that can be cooked in a microwave in one minute. You can even get hold of vegetarian haggis, which is made using flour, breadcrumbs, onion, butter, lentils, oatmeal, eggs, and vegetable stock.

Haggis is eaten all year round and often forms the focus of the evening meal on Saint Andrew's Day. But of course it is on Burns' Night that the haggis is particularly celebrated.

WHY DO SCOTS CELEBRATE
BURNS' NIGHT?

On 25 January, Scots all over the world gather together to honor the short, yet prolific, career of their national poet, Robert Burns, because 25 January is his birthday. Also known as the Ploughman Poet (because among other jobs he held, he had once worked as a ploughman), Burns was, and still is, Scotland's favorite poet. This is mainly due to the fact that he wrote in the same way that Scottish people spoke. He came from a humble background, but his natural talent made him a national hero.

Robert Burns was born in Alloway, in Ayrshire, in 1759, and was the eldest of seven children. Curiously, his father's name was William Burnes, and his mother's name was Agnes Broun. Today their gravestone spells their names "Burns" and "Brown," but the truth is they're actually on their third memorial. The first two were chipped to pieces by fans of the Ploughman Poet desperate to acquire souvenirs that had even the remotest connection to the great man or his family.

Burns' poetry was inspired by the stories his mother's old maid told him when he was a child. Indeed, the poet is quoted as saying, "She had the largest collection in the county of tales and songs concerning devils, ghosts, fairies, brownies, witches, warlocks, kelpies, elf-candles, wraiths, giants, enchanted towers, dragons and other nonsense. From this grew the seeds of my poetry."

Inspired by the old maid's tales, when he was old enough Burns traveled around Scotland, collecting old songs and ensuring that they were published before they could be forgotten by a declining oral society. However, he wasn't averse to changing lines here or there, or adding whole verses where he thought the originals needed pepping up a bit. There's now no way of telling which bits are the original

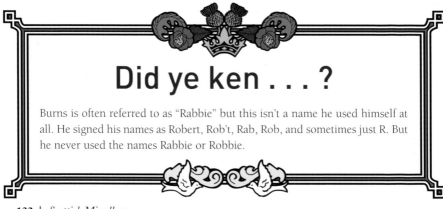

Did ye ken . . . ?

Burns is often referred to as "Rabbie" but this isn't a name he used himself at all. He signed his names as Robert, Rob't, Rab, Rob, and sometimes just R. But he never used the names Rabbie or Robbie.

Scottish folk songs and which are Burns' additions, such as with the classic "Auld Lang Syne."

Despite being only a humble ploughman, Burns was well educated. He read Shakespeare and used French and Latin in his letters. He was also a competent fiddler and could sight-read music. He became a theater enthusiast and was planning to write a play just before he died.

Regardless of the success and popularity he enjoyed while he was alive, Burns was never a rich man. He worked as a farmer, but his holding was on poor ground and didn't turn a profit. He took a job as an officer with the customs service, becoming an exciseman, charged with tracking down and putting a stop to smugglers and the like. In July 1796 he was forced to write to his publisher and beg him for money: "I implore you for five pounds. I owe the money to a cruel scoundrel of a shopkeeper who has taken it into his head that I am dying. Do, for God's sake, send me that sum. The horrors of jail have made me half-mad."

As it turned out, the shopkeeper was right. Burns was very ill. After enjoying a few drinks with friends, he started on his way home but fell asleep on the roadside before he ever made it to his door. It was his roadside nighttime nap that probably ended up giving him rheumatic fever, and Burns died two weeks later. He was thirty-seven years old. Around ten thousand people attended his burial.

Ten Things You Didn't Know About Robert Burns

1. The first Burns' Supper on record took place in Alloway in 1801, when a group of the poet's friends gathered in July—not January—to mark the fifth anniversary of his death.

2. After that Burns' Suppers were held on 29 January, as opposed to 25 January as they are now, because his friends got his birthday wrong! It was only after double-checking the church register that 25 January became the definitive date.

3. Burns lived life to the fullest, and there is some speculation as to the number of children he fathered. It is commonly accepted that he had twelve children by four different mothers, but it could actually have been as many as fourteen children by six different women. (He surely liked to sow his wild porridge oats!) His youngest son, Maxwell, was born on the day Burns was buried.

4. Burns once famously said, "I'll be damned if I ever write for money." (Not all of us can afford to be so proud!)

5. His first book of published poems was a great success, and when he visited Edinburgh on 28 November 1786, the gates of the city were flung open to him.

6. Burns was not a heavy drinker, even though his poems might suggest otherwise; neither his health nor his wallet would have allowed it.

7. The 224-line poem "Tam o' Shanter" was drafted in a single day while Burns was occupied on his day job.

8. Burns' poems have been published in over twenty-four languages, including Esperanto—the artificial language based on words common to all European languages.

9. It is estimated that Robert Burns is now worth £100 million in tourist revenue alone. On top of that, he's believed to be responsible for another $8.3 million of High Street sales and $1.8 million of sales of traditional food.

10. More people will take part in a Burns' Supper each year than the total population of Scotland at the time of Burns' birth!

Burns' Suppers, which form the focus of Burns' Night celebrations, can be either casual affairs or something much more formal. However, whatever their nature, the basic format varies very little. On arriving guests should be offered a drink (usually whisky) and once they are all seated at table, the chairman makes his welcome. This is followed by the Selkirk Grace and then the banquet begins.

The Selkirk Grace

Some hae meat and canna eat,
And some wad eat that want it,
But we hae meat and we can eat,
And sae the Lord be thankit.

Burns' Supper Menu

Cock-a-Leekie Soup *or* Cullen Skink
Haggis, Neeps, and Champit Tatties
Cranachan *or* Sherry Trifle

After the first course has been cleared away, the haggis will be piped in—the chef carrying it to the table, accompanied by a piper playing a stirring Scottish tune—and the chairman, or another esteemed guest, will give the "Address to a Haggis." Reciting the words of Burns' poem with gusto, the speaker plunges a knife into the haggis at the words:

"An' cut you up wi' ready slight
Trenching your gushing entrails bright
Like onie ditch."

The address over, the guests toast the haggis and the health of the poet, with a wee dram of whisky. When the meal is finished, the chairman (or esteemed guest) makes the first speech, "The Immortal Memory," which pays tribute to the life and work of Robert Burns. This is followed by the "Toast to the Lasses," a lighthearted tribute to all the ladies present that should be humorous, but never unkind. An elected female member of the party then gives "The Lasses' Response." The formalities over, the rest of the night is spent enjoying the songs and poems of Burns, as performed by the guests themselves.

Among Robert Burns' best-known works are "Auld Lang Syne," "My Love is Like a Red, Red Rose," "Tae a Mouse," and "Tam O' Shanter."

A traditional tam-o'-shanter is a Scottish bonnet worn by men and named after the eponymous hero of Burns' famous poem. The bonnet is made of wool with a toorie (or bobble) in the center. The crown is roughly twice the diameter of the head. Originally they only came in blue and, as a result, were called "blue bonnets."

The different battalions of the Royal Regiment of Scotland identify themselves by wearing distinctively colored hackles (plumes of feathers) on their tam-o'-shanters, while soldiers of the Black Watch of Canada wear a red hackle on both their duty tam-o'- shanters and dress balmorals (or Balmoral Bonnet, another traditional Scottish cap worn with Highland Dress). In many regiments it is traditional for soldiers to wear a tam-o'-shanter, while officers (and sometimes senior noncommissioned officers) wear the balmoral or Glengarry (a boat-shaped cap without a peak, made of thick-milled woollen material with a toorie on top and ribbons hanging down behind) instead.

However, Burns' narrative poem "Tam o' Shanter," published in 1791, tells the story of a man who stayed too long at a public house and witnessed a disturbing vision on his way home. Tam o' Shanter, the boozy hero of the tale, upon reaching

Did ye ken . . . ?

The well-known Scottish landmark, the thirteenth-century Bridge of Doon (also known as the "Brig o' Doon"), gave its name to the musical *Brigadoon*, which tells the supernatural tale of a mysterious Scottish village that appears for only one day every hundred years. No one from Brigadoon may ever leave, or the enchantment will be broken, and the village will disappear into the mist forever. Two American tourists, lost in the Scottish Highlands, come across the village just as a wedding is about to be celebrated, and consequently their arrival has serious implications for the village's inhabitants.

The original production opened on Broadway in 1947 and ran for 581 performances before transferring across the pond to London's West End.

Alloway kirk at the wizarding hour, witnesses a coven of witches dancing around their old, sooty black-guard master, who was keeping them all alive through the power of his bagpipe. Fleeing the scene on his old nag, Meg, he is chased by the witches as far as the Bridge over the River Doon. Unable to cross running water, the hags have no choice but to let old Tam escape.

The plot of "Tam o' Shanter" can be summarized in two holoalphabetic sentences, meaning that every letter of the alphabet is used at least once in each sentence, as in the better known example, "The quick brown fox jumps over a lazy dog."

Tam, jesting, boozes quickly while vexed wife pouts wrathfully.

Tam gawps at devilish frenzy but jumping mare forces quick exit.

If you feel inspired by Burns' poetry and would like to try hosting your own Burns' Night supper, you might like to try the following recipes out on your guests. The first two are starters, while cranachan is a delicious sweet dessert, sometimes called cream crowdie.

COCK-A-LEEKIE SOUP

1 chicken (or several pieces of uncooked and boned chicken wings, legs or quarters)
14 oz. (400 g) leeks
4 oz. (100 g) precooked, stoned prunes
1 oz. (25 g) of rice
3½ pints water or soup stock
1 tsp. brown sugar
Salt and pepper, 1 bay leaf, and some thyme
Parsley to garnish

Place the chicken in a pot and add the soup stock or water. Bring it to a boil, and remove and discard any fatty scum that appears at the top of the pot. Wash the leeks and roughly chop them into about 1-inch (2-cm) pieces, using the green and white pieces.

Once the chicken has been boiling for 1 hour, add the leeks, the bay leaf, and the thyme. Bring it back to a boil and simmer for 2 hours. Season with salt and pepper.

Cullen Skink

1 smoked haddock
Water
1 onion
Mashed potato
25g butter
1 pint (600 ml) milk
Salt and pepper

Skin the smoked haddock, and add just enough boiling water to cover. Bring back to the boil and add the chopped onion. Once it's cooked, take the haddock out and debone it, remembering also to remove the head and tail. Break the fish up into a dish, and return the bones to the pot, boiling them another hour. Strain the stock and put back to a boil once more. Boil the milk in a separate pot before adding it to the stock along with the fish. Add the salt and boil for several minutes, and then add the mashed potato until you achieve a nice consistency. Finally, add the butter and pepper and serve.

Cranachan

2½ oz. (60 g) medium oatmeal
5 oz. (150 g) raspberries
4 tbs malt whisky
4 tbs runny Scottish honey
1 pint (600 ml) double cream
1 oz. (25 g) soft brown sugar (if desired)

Scatter the oatmeal onto a baking tray and toast in a low oven or under the grill until they become golden brown. (Adding a half measure of soft brown sugar to the oatmeal while toasting it will give it a crunchy texture and caramel flavor.)

Blend 2 oz. (50 g) of the raspberries in a food processor until they become smooth. Whip the double cream until a stiff mixture forms, then stir in the honey and whisky, and mix well. Fold in 2 oz. (50 g) of the toasted oatmeal, then fold in the raspberry puree. A rippled effect should be achieved.

Spoon the mixture into tall glasses or individual serving dishes. Scatter the remaining oatmeal and raspberries on the top of each dish. (You may toss the raspberries in whisky and warm honey before serving to achieve an enhanced flavor.) Serve and enjoy.

WHO LIVES IN BALMORAL CASTLE?

Balmoral Castle, and its accompanying estate, is set within the magnificent scenery of Royal Deeside, Aberdeenshire, in the shadows of Lochnagar (which is both the name of a loch, "the loch of the goat," and a hill, also known as the White Mounth). The whole estate extends to just over 50,000 acres, and includes heather-clad hills, alongside ancient Caledonian woodland and the beautiful River Dee itself, as well as seven Munros.

Today it remains the personal property and summer holiday residence of the sovereign (the queen was in residence at Balmoral when Diana, Princess of Wales died in August 1997), but it has not always been so, despite having been associated with royalty since the time of Robert the Bruce in the 1300s and owned by King Robert II (1316–90), who had a hunting lodge in the area.

The Balmoral Estate began as a home built by Sir William Drummond in 1390. By the seventeenth century it was owned by the Gordons of Huntly, but in 1662 it passed into the hands of the Farquarsons of Inverey. In 1798 it came into the possession of the Duff banking clan—Earles of Fife—as part of a settlement of debts, but it was their lessee, Sir Robert Gordon, whose hospitality resulted in the estate coming to the attention of Queen Victoria.

Twenty years after her uncle, William IV, visited Scotland, Victoria and her husband, Prince Albert of Saxe-Coburg, and Gotha, made their first trip to the Scottish Highlands. So taken were they with the beauty of Britain's last wilderness, and Balmoral in particular, after Gordon's death in 1848 the queen and prince consort took over the lease.

Victoria and Albert bought Balmoral Castle and its estate outright in 1852 for 30,000 guineas, after its owner choked to death on a fishbone. At Albert's request, a local architect, William Smith, city architect of Aberdeen, was hired to remodel the estate in the Scots Baronial style. The castle that originally stood on the site was

Did ye ken . . . ?

As well as the overview it offers of the Balmoral estate, the hill Lochnagar (actually an outlier of the Cairngorms) has a number of other royal connections. In 1861, Queen Victoria herself attempted to ascend to its summit, while in 1980 His Royal Highness Prince Charles, the Prince of Wales, published a children's book called *The Old Man of Lochnagar*. He originally wrote it to amuse his younger brothers, which, considering its intended audience, might explain why during the course of the story, the Old Man spends so much of his time without any clothes on.

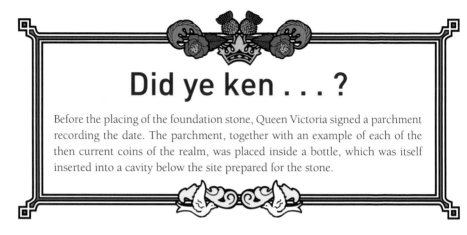

Did ye ken . . . ?

Before the placing of the foundation stone, Queen Victoria signed a parchment recording the date. The parchment, together with an example of each of the then current coins of the realm, was placed inside a bottle, which was itself inserted into a cavity below the site prepared for the stone.

deemed to be too small for the needs of Victoria and Albert's extensive family. Under the supervision of the prince consort, a new building was designed.

A new site was chosen, a hundred yards to the northwest of the existing castle, so that the Royal Family could continue to occupy the old house while their new home was being built. The foundation stone for Balmoral Castle was laid by Queen Victoria on 28 September 1853 and can be found at the foot of the wall adjacent to the west face of the entrance porch.

Balmoral Castle was completed in 1856, at which point the old building was knocked down. The original building is commemorated by a stone, which marks the position of the front door to the demolished castle and which is located on the front lawn at a point opposite the tower, about a hundred yards from the path.

This new castle was built from granite quarried from neighboring Glen Gelder, which produced a nearly white stone known as pale gray ashlar. Prince Albert took care of the interior design himself, using the red Royal Stewart and the green Hunting Stewart tartans for carpets. The Dress Stewart was used for curtains and upholstery.

Did ye ken . . . ?

According to the Scottish Tartans Authority, the Balmoral tartan should only be worn by members of the British Royal Family.

Victoria and Albert were smitten with the Highlands and spent a significant amount of their time at Balmoral. They hosted many Highland activities. Victoria herself was frequently attended by pipers while her children wore Highland dress. Prince Albert enjoyed watching the Highland games. However, as the craze for these games swept Scotland, the Highland population itself suffered terribly as a result of the Highland Clearances.

In her personal journals Queen Victoria described Balmoral as, "my dear paradise in the Highlands." When she died in 1901, under the terms of her will, the Balmoral Estate passed to her eldest son, the new King Edward VII, and it has continued to be passed down through the British Royal Family to the current Queen Elizabeth II.

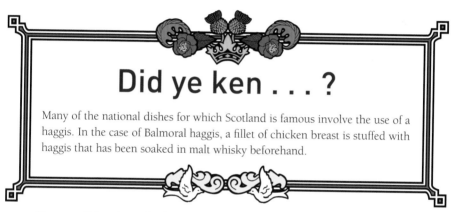

Did ye ken . . . ?

Many of the national dishes for which Scotland is famous involve the use of a haggis. In the case of Balmoral haggis, a fillet of chicken breast is stuffed with haggis that has been soaked in malt whisky beforehand.

Because it has been in the possession of the royal family for more than 150 years, the natural beauty of the estate—its flora and fauna as well as its rugged landscapes—along with the Scots Baronial architecture of the castle itself, have been preserved.

Balmoral has been more than just a favorite home for Queen Victoria and her descendants. Even today it remains largely as it was in Victoria's time, and successive royal owners have followed the Prince Albert's example and have continued to make improvements to the estate. The queen, the duke of Edinburgh, and the prince of Wales all take a close personal interest in the running, maintaining, and improvement of the estate. Indeed, one of the estate's most ecologically important areas is the 2,500-acre Ballochbuie Forest, bought in

1878 by Queen Victoria to save it from a timber merchant. Ballochbuie now contains one of the largest remnants of native Caledonian pine forest left in the entire country.

The castle grounds themselves are well endowed with all manner of cairns, statues, and even cottages that commemorate various members of the royal family.

Balmoral is a working estate, occupying over 20,000 hectares of land. Deer stalking, grouse shooting, forestry, and farming are the main land uses, while parts of the castle, gardens, and exhibitions are open to the public between April and July. The estate includes 2,940 hectares of grouse moor, 3,000 hectares of forest (including Ballochbuie), and 222 hectares of arable farmland or pasture. Those animals that are reared and tended on the estate include one hundred Highland cattle, and the queen's Highland, Fell, and Haflinger ponies. The queen founded the Balmoral fold of Highland Cattle in 1953 and it now has twenty-nine cows, while more than twenty ponies are kept for trekking and deer retrieval during the stalking season. Several thousand red deer also called the estate grounds home.

The estate provides for and works with the local community, employing fifty full-time staff and fifty to one hundred on a part-time basis, particularly when the queen makes her annual visit. On top of this, around four thousand people are employed in the tourist industry on Deeside and the surrounding area, with Balmoral one of the star attractions for visitors. Some 85,000 people visit the castle and gardens each year. Many others enjoy the spectacular scenery that forms part of Balmoral, with four full-time rangers conducting public walks during the summer to particular sites of interest on the estate.

Ultimately, in answer to the question "Who lives in Balmoral Castle?," it is the various staff—housekeepers, cleaners, butlers, gardeners, estate managers, game-keepers, and all the rest—who really call the castle home year-round.

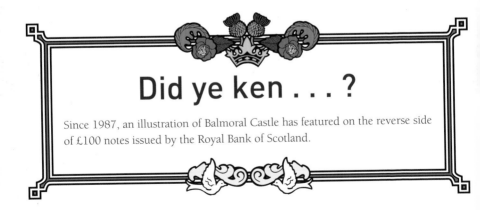

Did ye ken . . . ?

Since 1987, an illustration of Balmoral Castle has featured on the reverse side of £100 notes issued by the Royal Bank of Scotland.

IS THERE REALLY A MONSTER
LIVING IN LOCH NESS?

I t's one of the world's most enduring mysteries and still sends cryptozoologists into the Highlands of Scotland—along with several thousand tourists—on an annual basis. But is there really a prehistoric monster, forgotten by both time and evolution, living in Loch Ness?

More than twenty-two miles long, Loch Ness is the longest British lake and holds the greatest volume of water of any lake in Britain, more than the contents of all the other lakes and reservoirs in England combined! It is effectively a huge fissure, scoured out by glaciers during the last ice age, that cuts a great divide along the Great Glen, Glen Mor. In places, the loch is more than 700 feet deep, with an average depth of more than 400 feet, leading many people to believe that it would make the perfect place to hide a monster.

The area around Loch Ness has been settled since at least 2,000 BC, although the first mention of a monster in a written source doesn't appear until the sixth century AD and involves our old friend Saint Columba. Adamnan, the chronicler of the saint's life, tells of an incident that occurred while Columba was traveling to Inverness to meet Brude, King of the Picts.

Saint Columba and the Waterhorse

While traveling the Highlands of Scotland, preaching to the pagan tribesmen, Saint Columba found it necessary to cross the River Ness. Arriving safely at the bank of the river, he came across a group of local people burying a victim of the water monster that was said to dwell within the loch. The wretched individual had been attacked by the beastie and died from his wounds.

The dead man's boat was still out on the loch, so the saint instructed one of his companions to swim out and drag it back in. However, no sooner was the man in the water than the monster rose from the bottom of the lake and seized the monk in its jaws, intending to devour him whole. Saint Columba made the sign of the cross and shouted at the creature, commanding it to be gone. The effect was instantaneous; the monster released its prey and quickly made off in the opposite direction.

Did ye ken . . . ?

In 1941, during World War II, an Italian newspaper reported that the bombing of Scotland had been so heavy that the Loch Ness monster had been killed by a direct hit. But it wasn't true—it was only Nazi propaganda—and Nessie turned up again after the war, when people started holidaying in the area again in the mid-1950s.

Did ye ken . . . ?

Loch Ness isn't the only Scottish loch rumored to have its own resident beastie. There are others, including Morag, the monster of Loch Morar; Archie of Loch Arkaig; Lizzie of Loch Lochy; Wee Oichy of Loch Oich; and Quiochy of Loch Quoich. On top of those, there are another sixteen lochs where strange creatures have allegedly been sighted.

According to some versions of the tale, the monk died, and the saint then brought him back to life. Occasional reports of sightings of the waterhorse surfaced down through the centuries until the modern legend began to take shape in 1933, more than 1,300 years after Columba's encounter with the beast, when a new road was constructed along the northern bank of the loch, making it more accessible to visitors. In May of that year, Mr. and Mrs. McKay, who had been out in their car on the new road, reported seeing "an enormous animal rolling and plunging on the surface." When the story was reported in the *Daily Mail*, it was introduced with the headline: MONSTER OF LOCH NESS IS NOT LEGEND BUT A FACT.

Sightings of Nessie, as the monster was nicknamed, steadily increased from that point on. Some people claimed that the monster resembled a plesiosaur, a 40-foot (12-meter) reptile from the age of the dinosaurs. Others said it was like a huge snake. Various photographs were taken that revealed dark shapes on the surface. In the 1970s, an under-water photo showed a bulky shape with what appeared to be a diamond-shaped "flipper." Other examples of so-called photographic evidence have been exposed as fakes, and some that apparently show humps breaking the surface may simply be pictures or footage of waves, otters, floating logs, and fish.

Despite hundreds of sightings, all manner of supposed evidence, theories, and scientific expeditions, no one has yet

Is there really a monster living in Loch Ness? | **145**

been able to prove that Nessie really exists. Recent expeditions using submarines and sonar even failed to locate the monster. Tourists still flock to Loch Ness and even take helicopter rides in the hope of spotting the waterhorse for themselves.

That there are so many legends of great worms, waterhorses, and kelpies in Scottish folklore may be due to the fact that most Scottish Highlanders lived near areas of deep water and, because it was such a part of their life, took a great deal of interest in it. The kelpie turns up in different shapes and colors and in different places, but the Great Waterhorse of Loch Ness was said to be particularly large and black. Most sightings of the beast have been from Urquhart Castle, the ruin of a medieval castle that stands on a promontory halfway along the northern shore of the loch, close to where the waters are at their deepest.

Reports of the elusive monster said to live in Loch Ness's forbidding waters are still to be found in newspapers at least once or twice a year, and you will always find at least one monster-hunting expedition lurking at the edge of the loch with long-range telescopes and sounding equipment at the ready, just in case.

HOW DO CURLING AND SHINTY DIFFER?

Curling is a team sport in which stones are slid across a sheet of carefully prepared flat ice toward a target area. It is related to bowls, boule, and shuffleboard. Two teams of four players take turns to slide heavy, polished, blue hone granite stones across the curling sheet toward a circular target called the house. Each team has eight stones, and the purpose is to accumulate the highest score for a game. Points are scored for the stones resting closest to the center of the house at the conclusion of each end. An end is completed when both teams have thrown all of their stones.

Shinty is one of the fastest and, supposedly, most physically demanding and skillful sports in the world. It is played outdoors on a pitch 140 to 170 yards long. Shinty is also a team game, with two opposing teams of players trying to play a small leather ball with a curved stick, known as a caman, into goals (or hails) erected at the ends of the pitch. The game is traditionally played on grass, although since 2009 it has also been played on Astroturf.

Curling has been described as the "Roarin' Game," the roar being the noise made by the granite stones as they travel over the ice, and it is widely believed to be one of the world's oldest team sports. Curling is thought to have been invented in late medieval Scotland, and the first written reference to something like a curling contest comes from the records of Paisley Abbey, Renfrewshire, and is dated February 1541. Two paintings by Pieter Bruegel the Elder (dated 1565) show Dutch peasants curling, but then this shouldn't be seen as being too surprising, since Scotland and the Low Countries had strong trading and cultural links in the sixteenth century.

Two curling stones were uncovered in Scotland when an old pond was drained at Dunblane; one was inscribed with the date 1511, and the other 1551. The word "curling" first appeared in print in 1620 in Perth, in the preface and the verses of a poem by Henry Adamson.

The first playing stones (or "rocks," as they are also called) were flat-bottomed river stones that were sometimes notched or even shaped. This meant that the thrower had little control over the stone, and relied on luck rather than skill to win a game. However, the weavers of East Ayrshire relaxed by playing curling matches,

Did ye ken . . . ?

Curling stones are traditionally made from Ailsa Craig granite. They weigh approximately forty-two pounds.

Did ye ken . . . ?

In the past, specially built curling houses weres used in Scotland and elsewhere to store curling stones, brushes, and the equipment used to maintain curling ponds. These houses were relatively small and often located in isolated places, although some belonged to larger country estates and, as a consequence, were much grander in appearance. Easier transportation, the establishment of ice rinks, and a warmer climate are all factors that have resulted in the demise of the curling house, and most have been demolished or allowed to fall into ruin.

and the stones they used were the heavy stone weights from their looms, fitted with a detachable handle especially for the purpose. In these early days of the game, it was played on frozen lochs and ponds.

Outdoor curling grew in popularity between the sixteenth and nineteenth centuries, the Scottish climate at the time producing reliably icy conditions each winter. Kilsyth Curling Club claims to be the first club in the world. Formally constituted in 1716, it is still in existence today. Kilsyth also claims to possess the oldest purpose-built curling pond in the world. The first rules were drawn up in Scotland and formally adopted in 1838.

As you would probably expect, Scotland is home to the World Curling Federation, the international governing body for curling, which is based in Perth. However, in our modern age, the game is most firmly established in Canada, having been taken there originally by Scottish immigrants. The Royal Montreal Curling Club is the oldest established sports club still active in North America; it was established in 1807. The first curling club in the United States, the Orchard Lake Curling Club (based thirty miles from Detroit), was not formed until 1830. By the end of the nineteenth century, the game had been introduced to Switzerland as well as Sweden. Today, curling is popular across Europe (especially in Norway and Finland) and has even spread as far as China, Korea, Japan, Australia, and New Zealand.

The first world curling championship, the Scotch Cup, was only open to men. In Falkirk and Edinburgh in 1959, the first world title was won by the Canadian team from Regina, Saskatchewan.

Curling began on the path to becoming an Olympic sport at the first Olympic Winter Games, held in Chamonix in 1924. In 1932 at Lake Placid, curling was listed as a demonstration sport, and it would be another twenty-five years before a meeting was held in Edinburgh, in 1957, to discuss forming an international organization, which would be necessary for the sport to be awarded Olympic medal status. It may surprise you to learn that curling has only been an official sport in the Winter Olympic Games since 1998!

Shinty is one of the oldest games in the world. Throughout recorded history, it seems that every civilization has played a game with a club and a ball. The game pangea, as described by Roman scribes, would appear to be the progenitor of modern hockey, hurling, and shinty.

Shinty (called *iomain* or *camanachd* in Gaelic) evolved in the Highlands of Scotland, although it was introduced by the Gaels, who came from Ireland, over two thousand years ago, along with Christianity. It is now played all over Scotland, as well as in the United States. Shinty is similar to games like hockey and lacrosse, although, unlike in those games, the feet can be used to stop the ball. (Only goalkeepers are allowed to use their hands.) There is no restriction on the swing of the *caman* (which is the Gaelic word for "stick," appropriately enough). Players can strike the ball with both sides of the stick, as in ice hockey. It is fast-moving game, with the ball being hit around the field of play at speeds over 100 mph.

The caman was originally made of ash or hickory cut from a tree with a natural bend, although in Uist, stalks of seaweed were put to use due to a lack of trees growing there. The ball is about the size of a tennis ball. The interior, of cork and worsted, is covered with leather, or a similar approved material, although originally blocks of wood, solid pieces of cork, and even bone were used instead.

The origins of the name "shinty" are unclear but there is one theory that it derived from the cries used in the game, such as "shin ye," "shin you," and "shin t'ye." Other dialect names for the game include shinnins, shinnack, and shinnup. It was traditionally played throughout the winter months. On New Year's Day whole villages would gather together to compete in matches with teams of up to several hundred a side.

Did ye ken . . . ?

Hurling, a game not unlike shinty, is played in Ireland. It uses different sticks that have a broader face. However, there often are matches organized between shinty and hurling teams. The first such games were played in 1897 in Glasgow, and challenges regularly take place now at the club level, particularly during the summer months.

Shinty is still a truly amateur sport, and is a community game that is played in some of the remotest parts of Scotland. The Dell playing fields at Kinguisse are thought to be the original home of organized shinty as it is known today. The main shinty-playing areas are Argyll, Lochaber, the Eastern Highlands, and Skye, and most cities also support at least one team in the leagues. The Camanachd Association, based in Inverness, is the governing body for shinty around the world.

The Glenmorangie Camanachd Cup Knock Out Championship was first played in 1896 and won by Kingussie. It is an annual event, and the cup final, which attracts crowds of between three thousand and five thousand, is customarily played on the first Saturday in June.

London Camanachd is now the only shinty club in England, although the game was once played widely in England in the nineteenth and early twentieth centuries. Indeed, Nottingham Forest Football Club was originally established by shinty players. London Camanachd has historically been attached to Scotland's South District league. They played the first officially recognized shinty match outside Scotland in eighty years, on Saturday 22 July 2006, against the Highlanders.

Shinty is also currently enjoying a revival in North America. Teams such as the Northern California Camanachd Club (or NCCC) now play at Highland Games and other venues across the United States.

More widespread and popular than shinty is football (soccer), with most areas participating in local leagues. However, in September 2009, the Scottish comedian Billy Connolly suggested that shinty should become Scotland's national sport, because the country's football team's performances had been so dire.

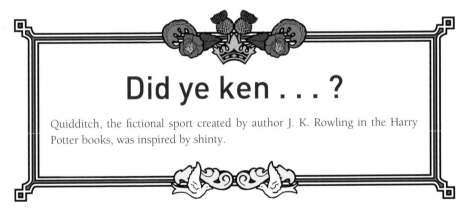

Did ye ken . . . ?

Quidditch, the fictional sport created by author J. K. Rowling in the Harry Potter books, was inspired by shinty.

WHY IS KING ARTHUR'S SEAT IN EDINBURGH?

Arthur's Seat is the name given to a rugged hill 850 feet (250 meters) tall that stands in Holyrood Park, adjacent to Holyrood Palace in Edinburgh. The Once and Future King is said to lie within a cavern beneath the mountain, not dead but sleeping, with his noble knights about him. However, the name "Arthur's Seat" is also attached to a number of other elevations (in Australia, India, and New Zealand). The name Arthur's Seat in this case is probably a corruption of Archer's Seat, since the area has been a royal hunting ground since at least the twelfth century.

Arthur's Seat in Edinburgh is part of Salisburg Crags, the dramatic profile of which can be seen from many miles away. The hill is actually an extinct volcano that last blew its top some 350 million years ago. However, the connections with Arthur persist. In Arthurian times (in other words, the Dark Ages following the Roman exodus from Great Britain), Scotland was divided among three peoples—the Britons in the Lowlands and, north of Hadrian's Wall, the Picts and Scots.

Different Arthurian scholars have differing ideas as to who was actually in charge in Scotland in Arthur's time. Geoffrey of Monmouth says that Scotland was ruled in Arthur's time by King Auguselus, but according to Hector Boece in the *Scotorum Historiae*, the king of the Scots was Eugenius, an ally of Mordred, Arthur's bastard son. The *Historia Meriadoci* makes Urien the King of the Scots.

Historically, of course, the kings of the Hiberno-Scottish kingdom of Dalriada at this time were Fergus More, Domangort, Comgall, and Gabran, but their actual dates are uncertain. It is rather more difficult to discover who was ruling the Britons of Strathclyde at the time, as reliable lists do not exist.

Edinburgh is not the only place in Scotland associated with King Arthur. There is Arthur's O'on near Falkirk, which is really a Roman temple dating from the second century AD. It was pulled down in 1743, but the dovecote at Penicuick House, which stands nearby, was built as a replica of it. Arthur is also supposed to have fought a battle at Cat Coit Celidon, the region called *Silva Caledoniae* in Latin (or "Wood

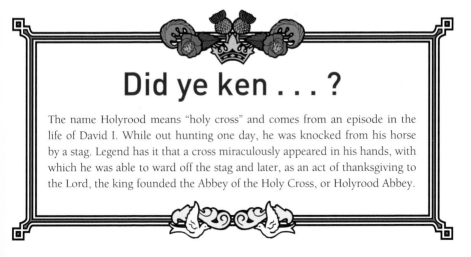

Did ye ken . . . ?

The name Holyrood means "holy cross" and comes from an episode in the life of David I. While out hunting one day, he was knocked from his horse by a stag. Legend has it that a cross miraculously appeared in his hands, with which he was able to ward off the stag and later, as an act of thanksgiving to the Lord, the king founded the Abbey of the Holy Cross, or Holyrood Abbey.

of Scotland"), and another at the River Tribuit, which is also purported to be in Scotland. Arthur's Seat in Edinburgh is the best known of all of these curious monuments to the Once and Future King.

Edinburgh, sometimes called the "Athens of the North," has been inhabited in one form or another since prehistoric times. It was first mentioned in the seventh century, when a British bard who was there around the year AD 600 wrote a poem describing the young warriors of Eidin feasting and preparing for battle. When the Anglo-Saxons invaded Britain, the Angle tribe established the kingdom of Northumbria (meaning the land "north of the Humber") and from there spread west to Chester and north as far as the Firth of Forth. On a hill near the sea they came upon the fort of Eidin and ultimately captured it. They held onto it for a long time, adding their own -burg (meaning "fortified town") to the name of the place and so Edinburgh, as we know it today, was born.

The Gaels, who joined together the different races of the north into one kingdom, eventually drove the Northumbrians out of Edinburgh. In the Gaelic language a castle was a *dun*, and the Gaels called this particular castle Dun Edin, meaning "fort on the sloping ridge." To the large numbers of Angles who remained in the Lowlands it would always be Edinburgh.

Edinburgh grew up around its castle. The huddle of huts that first clustered around the castle rock gradually spread east. By 1532, Edinburgh was the capital of Scotland and by the seventeenth century, it was the most populated place in

Did ye ken . . . ?

In 1836, five young boys hunting rabbits on Arthur's Seat found seventeen miniature coffins hidden inside a cave. They were arranged under slates on three tiers, two tiers of eight with one solitary coffin on the top. Each coffin was only four inches in length and contained a tiny wooden figure, expertly carved, with painted black boots and custom-made clothes. The ones on the bottom tier appeared to have been there the longest, as they were more deteriorated than those placed above them. To this day, no one is quite sure what they are meant to represent. Suggestions have ranged from witches' voodoo dolls to good-luck charms carried by sailors, and one theory even has it that they are supposed to be the victims of William Burke and William Hare, the notorious Edinburgh murderers. They were kept in a private collection until 1901, when they were presented to the Museum of Scotland in Edinburgh. Only eight of them remain on display to the public today.

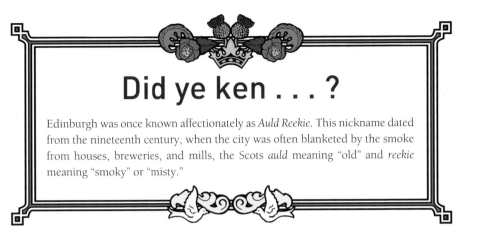

Did ye ken . . . ?

Edinburgh was once known affectionately as *Auld Reekie*. This nickname dated from the nineteenth century, when the city was often blanketed by the smoke from houses, breweries, and mills, the Scots *auld* meaning "old" and *reekie* meaning "smoky" or "misty."

Scotland. Its one major thoroughfare was the High Street, with the Grassmarket and Cowgate running roughly parallel and below it. Indeed the writer Daniel Defoe was inspired to write these words describing the High Street in 1724: "Perhaps the largest, longest and finest street for buildings and number of inhabitants, not only in Britain, but in the world."

Elsewhere, however, Edinburgh was a maze of narrow closes. In comparison to modern standards, seventeenth-century towns were dirty and smelly places; there was no sanitation, and waste was simply thrown straight out onto the street. So it was that on this crowded spine of land the buildings grew upward—often by as many as eight stories. City society was organized vertically, with the wealthy living close to the top, above all the filth and squalor, and the poor (who included widows, tanners, shoemakers, and tailors) right in among it at the bottom.

Here, the great townhouses of nobles, churchmen, and merchants existed cheek-by-jowl with the vast mass of the toiling poor. Some people enjoyed extravagant luxuries, but life for the majority was basic, noisy, dirty, precarious, and, above all, short. Slowly the rich began to distance themselves from all this squalor and deprivation. First of all they moved farther east, to the then more exclusive environment of the Canongate, until at last, in the late eighteenth century, they upped sticks and traveled north, to the purpose-built and appropriately named New Town.

Running the length of the spine of rock on which the Old Town is built is the High Street—part of the Royal Mile. A series of lanes and alleyways lead away from it, falling away to either side, and these are the "wynds" and "closes," which once had gates that could be locked at night to protect the inhabitants from thieves and vagabonds. The closes were often named as a simple description of the businesses or activities that took place there, as is quite clearly demonstrated in the naming of Bakehouse Close. Fleshmarket and Skinners Close were where the slaughtermen, butchers, and tanners worked, while lawyers carried on their business in Advocate's Close. Some were named after prominent citizens and even charismatic or noticeable residents. An example of this is in the naming of Mary King's Close.

Did ye ken . . . ?

During the seventeenth century, at the height of the plague, on 27 June 1645, John Craig of Mary King's Close was appointed gravedigger at Greyfriars churchyard. Like others of his trade he was well provisioned with spirits, ale, beer, wheatbread, and tobacco. A patent protection against the plague at this time was to wear a spider in a walnut shell around your neck. Perhaps John Craig hadn't heard of this example of preventative medicine, for a month later he was dead and his coffin ordered.

Ten Sights to See in Edinburgh

The Royal Mile
Holyrood House
Edinburgh Castle
Mary King's Close
Saint Giles Cathedral
Edinburgh University
Waverley Station
Princes Street
New Town
Greyfriars Churchyard and Greyfriars Bobby

Did ye ken . . . ?

Another sight worth seeing is the Scott Monument. At 200 ft (61 m) tall, it is the largest monument erected to any writer anywhere in the world. Sir Walter Scott was the most popular writer of his age, but not everybody was a fan. In fact, the American author Mark Twain blamed his "romanticization of battle" for the South's decision to fight the American Civil War!

WHAT IS MALT WHISKY?

Inspiring bold John Barleycorn!
What dangers thou canst make us scorn!
Wi' tippenny, we fear nae evil;
Wi' usquebae, we'll face the devil!

Whisky is known the world over as Scotland's national drink. Made in Scotland, this fiery, heart-warming spirit is now drunk all over the world, and is one of country's principal exports. It is to the Scots what champagne is to the French. However, despite its strong connections with Scotland, whisky wasn't invented there. It was actually invented in ancient China. It probably arrived in Ireland before it ever reached Scotland and was first distilled by monks, although archaeological excavations on the appropriately named island of Rum, in the mid-1980s, found spores and pollen suggesting that some form of alcoholic drink was made there some six thousand years ago.

The word "whisky" comes from the Gaelic *uisge beatha*—which was itself the Irish translation of the Latin *aqua vitae*, meaning "water of life"—and which was shortened to *usqua* or *usky*. Whisky had reached the court of James IV by 1500 and around this time the barbers and surgeons of Edinburgh were given the right to make and sell *aqua vitae*, or *usqua*.

The first tax on whisky was imposed by the Scots Parliament of 1644. At this time, most distilling took place amid countryside communities, on a small scale, in private stills. Households were allowed to make the spirit for their own use, but it was illegal to sell it on to anyone else. When the tax on whisky was initiated, illicit stills became more and more common, particularly in the Highlands, and they were not brought under control until the nineteenth century.

The whisky produced at this time, and in this way, was a fiery spirit of inconsistent quality, not acceptable to an English palate. However, a market for the stuff

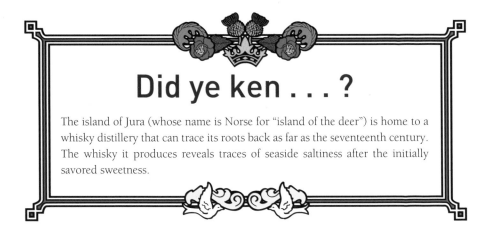

Did ye ken . . . ?

The island of Jura (whose name is Norse for "island of the deer") is home to a whisky distillery that can trace its roots back as far as the seventeenth century. The whisky it produces reveals traces of seaside saltiness after the initially savored sweetness.

Did ye ken . . . ?

Whisky is Scottish, but "Scotch" is whisky. Whiskey with an "e" is Irish, and bourbon is American whisky.

was created when the phylloxera epidemic hit European vineyards hard, resulting in a decrease in the production of not only wines but also brandy. Suddenly whisky was wanted, but it took a group of enterprising Scotsmen to recognize that a consistent whisky could best be produced by blending different types, notably malt and grain.

So how is whisky made, and what's the difference between malt whisky and grain whisky? Malt whisky is made from a watery extract of malted barley, fermented by yeast, and distilled in onion-shaped pot-stills, from which the alcohol is driven off by applying heat. To make malted barley, first the barley has to be steeped in water. In this state it is called green malt. This green malt is spread out over the floor of a kiln and dried by heat from a furnace fired by peat as well as coke. Differences in the peat and stream water used give each malt its own unique flavor.

After drying, the malt is ground into grist and mixed with water in a metal vat, or mash tun. The spirit that is produced at the end of the brewing process needs to mature in wooden casks (traditionally, sherry casks, although oak bourbon casks

Did ye ken . . . ?

Scots has numerous ways of describing someone who has enjoyed one too many single malts of an evening. They are said to be battered, bevvied, birlin', bleezin', blootered, faur-on, fleein', fou, guttered, hammered, jaiked up, leathered, miraculous, paralettic, pished, reekin', reelin', rubber, steamboats, steamin', stoatin', stocious, suitably refreshed, or tanked.

are now more readily available) for between eight to fifteen years! The longer the whisky is left to mature, the better quality (and more expensive) it will be. Most malt whisky will end up being blended with others, to produce a consistent taste, as well as price, but ninety to 100 single malts are bottled for drinking.

Grain whisky is a more recent invention, introduced in the 1830s. Made from corn and a little malted barley, the process of making grain whisky is much quicker and cheaper than malt distilling. The spirit in this way is also closer to pure alcohol. It is now produced in huge industrial plants, but it is rarely bottled to be drunk on its own. Instead, it is blended with other malt whiskies and actually forms the basis of most of the whisky on the market.

Some Scots would describe whisky as "smashin'" which is thought to have originated from the Gaelic expression 'S math sin meaning "that's good." Also, Drambuie (a golden liqueur based on Scotch whisky, sweetened with heather honey and flavored with herbs) comes from the Gaelic dram buidheach, meaning "the dram or drink that satisfies." Meanwhile, Glayva (the name of a popular brand) comes from the Gaelic for "very good," glè mhath.

Whisky is produced by distilleries throughout the Highlands and islands, but the island of Islay, with its seven distilleries, can legitimately claim the greatest concentration of production. Islay is renowned for its distinctive malt whiskies. However, the region of Speyside, in Aberdeenshire, where barley is widely grown, is where you will find more than half of Scotland's malt whisky distilleries. Indeed, the environment in which whisky is produced has as much a bearing on its character as how it is stored and how long it is left to mature.

Ten Top Scotch Whiskies

1. Glenmorangie—with a light, flowery taste and a strong distinctive perfume, it is the bestselling malt in Scotland.
2. The Macallan—aged in sherry casks and having a full flavor, it is the "Rolls Royce of Single Malts."
3. The Glenlivet—the most famous of the Speyside malts, it has been distilled since 1880.
4. Lagavulin—a classic whisky from the island of Islay, it has a dry, smoky palate.
5. Talisker—a single malt with an extremely hot, peppery flavor.
6. Lochnagar—a sweet whisky with sherry overtones, it is supposed to have been a favorite of Queen Victoria.
7. Highland Park—a whisky with a distinctive, aromatic, full-bodied, floral sweetness.
8. Edradour—comes from the smallest distillery in Scotland and is a delicious creamy and minty whisky.

9. Glenkinchie—straw-colored, sweetish, and with a fine floral nose, it is the most widely available Lowland single malt.
10. Famous Grouse—this is a very fine blended whisky, made using malts such as the Macallan and Highland Park.

Hot Toddy

1 tsp. sugar
1 tsp. Scottish heather honey
1 measure of Scotch whisky
boiling water

Place the sugar and honey in a warm glass. Add the whisky (preferably not a malt) and top it off with the boiling water. Stir gently with a silver spoon and then enjoy. It is said that a hot toddy like this will cure anything! Or, as the Irish proverb has it, "What whiskey will not cure, there is no cure for."

WELCOME!

TO
HALIFAX

WHAT DOES NOVA
SCOTIA HAVE TO DO WITH
SCOTLAND?

Nova Scotia is a province on the eastern seaboard of Canada. The name Nova Scotia is Latin and means "New Scotland." The peninsula was christened such by immigrants from the Highlands of Scotland who landed there more than two hundred years ago and found themselves confronted by a landscape that was amazingly similar to the one they had left behind on the other side of the Atlantic.

Many communities all around the world can trace their origin back to such Highland immigrants, but what makes Nova Scotia so special is that its present culture is still dominated by historic Gaelic traditions. The tens of thousands of Scottish and Irish immigrants who arrived throughout the eighteenth and nineteenth centuries really left their mark. Their Gaelic music, history, and language have endured in Nova Scotia for three centuries, and are still present in all aspects of everyday life in the province.

Shops sell kilts and road signs are in both English and Scottish Gaelic. In fact, it is the only region outside Scotland today where the Scots Gaelic language and culture live on. Those who speak Gaelic are referred to as Gaels, and there are more than two thousand Gaelic speakers in Nova Scotia today. In fact, you can still hear a Barra lilt on Gaelic spoken in Iona and Christmas Island, so strong are the region's links with the auld country.

The province of Nova Scotia is divided into two parts, Cape Breton Island and a much larger peninsula referred to as "the mainland." The former is linked to the latter by a narrow causeway. The mainland is connected to the rest of Canada by a fifteen-mile-wide stretch of land.

The capital of Nova Scotia is Halifax, a 258-year-old seaport that is home to more than a third of the province's population of 900,000. The city's Spring Garden Road is one of Canada's oldest and prettiest retail thoroughfares, and the region is in general known for its gracious Victorian architecture. The colorful fishing town of Lunenburg is a perfect surviving example of an early colonial town and is now classed as a UNESCO World Heritage site. It is also the home of Canada's world-famous tall ship the *Bluenose II*.

Did ye ken . . . ?

The world's highest tide ebb occurs out of the Minas Basin in the Bay of Fundy, in Nova Scotia. Burntcoat Head, located on the Noel Shore along the south side of the basin, is the location of the highest tidal range ever recorded on the planet.

Did ye ken . . . ?

Nova Scotia has its own annual Highland Games. Called the Antigonish Highland Games, they have been held every year since their inception in 1863.

Nova Scotia is known as well for its maritime culture as anything else. Circling rocky inlets and bays up and down the coast, you will see eagles, puffins, razorbills, and kittiwakes. Seafood is a specialty of the region, from lobster and Digby scallops to smoked cedar plank salmon to tasty clams. You will also find plump blueberries growing locally, as well as apples. The region is also becoming better known for its complex, full-bodied, and award-winning wines, including the famous Nova Scotia ice wine.

Nova Scotia possesses many exciting natural wonders that are just waiting to be discovered by the intrepid explorer. From the rugged Atlantic Coast and the lush, rich Annapolis Valley, which rolls down to the Nova Scotia Bay of Fundy, to the Northumberland Shore where the warmest waters north of Maine and long stretches of beach can be found, there really is something for everyone. Tourists, as well as

Did ye ken . . . ?

Alexander Graham Bell (1847–1922) came from a family of speech therapists, and having left his native Scotland to move to America opened a school near Boston to teach speech to deaf people. As Bell's assistant was testing microphones and receivers, he accidentally plucked at a wire, and Bell, working in the next room, heard the noise quite clearly. This led him to wonder whether speech could travel down the wire in the same way, and in 1876 Bell invented the telephone. He invested the money he made from various inventions in research into deafness.

locals, can take part in all manner of exciting outdoor activities from kayaking and hiking to whale watching and golfing.

Visitors to Cape Breton Island are often greeted with the words "Ciad mile failte," which means "a hundred thousand welcomes." It is there that you can truly explore the Celtic culture and history upon which Nova Scotia is founded. Cape Breton Island has its own Gaelic College of Celtic Arts and Crafts, a reconstructed Highland Village living history museum, and Celtic Music Interpretive Centre, not to mention the Celtic Colours International Festival, or you can take in the pageantry of Pipefest as part of the International Gathering of the Clans.

The Cabot Trail on Cape Breton Island (named after the fifteenth-century explorer John Cabot) is one of the most stunning stretches of highway in the world. Because Nova Scotia has 4,750 miles (7,600 kilometers) of coastline, there's certainly plenty to see. If you follow the Ceilidh Trail, you will come upon the Glenora Inn & Distillery, which produces North America's only single-malt whiskey, Glen Breton Rare.

Curiously, another well-known tourist attraction is the Alexander Graham Bell National Historic Site of Canada in Baddeck, on Cape Breton Island, where you can find out how Bell and his associates produced the fastest hydrofoil boat in the world as well as making improvements to the phonograph.

WHAT IS HOGMANAY, AND WHAT DOES "AULD LANG SYNE" REALLY MEAN?

In Scotland, the New Year celebrations are even more important than Christmas, so much so that they have their own unique name, "Hogmanay." *Hogmanay* is the name used to describe the New Year celebrations in Scotland, referring specifically to the date of 31 December but also to the gifts that are given and received on New Year's Eve.

Although people nowadays regard "Hogmanay" as being a peculiarly Scottish word, its origins are actually French. In Old French, the last day of the year was called *aguillanneuf*. In the northern French dialect *aguillanneuf* became *hoguinané*, and once it had traveled even farther north to Scotland, it had become Hogmanay.

As with the New Year celebrations of other cultures, the Scots Hogmanay has a number of traditions associated with it. Many people still believe that the house should be thoroughly cleaned on or before Hogmanay, in order to rid their homes of all the dirt collected in the Old Year and welcome the New Year into a clean home. (Of course whether or not you decide to clean before or after the New Year celebrations must surely depend on what sort of Hogmanay party you're planning.) Then, just before midnight, a window is opened at each side of the house to let the Old Year out and the New Year in.

After the New Year has been "brought in" at midnight, people go "first-footing" and pay the first visit of the year to friends and neighbors. In return, it is customary to welcome people into your home for a New Year's drink and a bite to eat. Ideally, to ensure good luck for the rest of the year, the first caller to your home after midnight on New Year's Day should be tall and dark-haired.

First-footers should always take a gift with them when calling upon their neighbors. Traditionally, these gifts should include a piece of coal, to bring warmth to the home, a bottle of whisky, and something to eat, to ensure that there will be plenty in the year to come. The first-footer was also supposed to wish everyone a happy New Year, and sometimes had to cut a special cake, stir the fire, or visit every room in the house. Some said that the first-footer should enter by the front door and leave by the back.

Although first-footing is now considered to be the archetypal Scottish custom, it used to be common in England and parts of Wales as well. The practice can only actually be traced back to the mid-nineteenth century. At the time, most householders who believed in the custom took it so seriously that they arranged beforehand with someone who fitted the positive stereotype for a first-footer to come along soon after midnight.

"Auld Lang Syne" is renowned as the world's most famous song that nobody knows. Traditionally, it is sung after the bells have rung at midnight on New Year's Day and everybody has been wished a happy New Year. "Auld Lang Syne" is no longer just a Scottish tradition either; it has become a staple part of New Year's celebrations the world over. But what do the words "Auld Lang Syne" mean, and where did the song originate?

Did ye ken . . . ?

The nineteenth-century Scottish writer John MacTaggart, author of *The Scottish Gallovidian Encyclopaedia*, had his own theory about the origin and meaning of the word Hogmanay. In 1824 he wrote:

I think *hog-ma-nay* means *hug-me-now*. Kissing, long ago, was a thing much more common than at present . . . on the happy nights of *hog-ma-nay* the kissing trade is extremely brisk, particularly in Auld Reekie; then the lasses must kiss with all the stranger lads they meet, while phrases not unlike to "John, come kiss me now" or "John, come hug me now" are frequently heard. From such causes, methinks, *hog-ma-nay* has started. The *hugging* day, the time to *hug-me-now*.

The expression *auld lang syne* is another way of saying that something happened a long time ago, in the olden days (as in "old long since"). Contrary to popular belief—a belief upheld by many Scottish people, as it turns out—the celebrated Scots poet and songwriter Robert Burns did not write the song. Neither did he ever claim that he had written it, even though he was the one to first write it down having heard it sung by someone else. That said, many of the words of the version that is best known today *are* thought to have been composed by Burns himself.

Indeed, some scholars believe that there is compelling evidence that Burns did in fact write and edit a large part of what became his version of "Auld Lang Syne," and that he himself put it into people's heads that he had overheard it sung by another. Certainly there is an older written version called "Should Auld Acquaintance be Foryett," which can be found in the Bannatyne Manuscript of 1568.

In spite of the fact that everybody would appear to be familiar with "Auld Lang Syne," relatively few people know all the words. In the early minutes of the New Year, all over Scotland and in other countries too, thousands of people get them wrong, or mumble verses, as they have no idea what the words should really be—although, admittedly, few of them really care. It is undoubtedly a song that is appreciated more for its sentiment than for its poetry.

In case you're planning to sing "Auld Lang Syne" yourself this coming New Year, reproduced below for your edification are all the words of the song.

Did ye ken . . . ?

As the basic tenet behind the custom of first-footing is to bring good luck into the home for the next twelve months, it is important that the first-footer conforms to the idea of what is considered "lucky," which basically means they have to be tall, dark, and handsome. However, those considered to be "unlucky" when it comes to first-footing (at least according to a late nineteenth-century Scottish source) include people who are pious and sanctimonious, flat-footed, barefooted, stingy, lame, who have a blind eye, who are midwives, women in general, ministers, doctors, grave diggers, thieves, those who have met with an accident on the way, and people carrying a knife or pointed tool. The underlying principles are clear—the first-footer must be whole, socially acceptable, and lucky, to guarantee those desirable qualities for the house for the forthcoming year.

I
Should auld acquaintance be forgot,
And never brought to mind?
Should auld acquaintance be forgot
And days of auld lang syne.
Chorus
For auld lang syne, my jo,
For auld lang syne,
We'll tak' a cup o' kindness yet,
For auld lang syne.

II
And surely ye'll be your pint-stoup
And surely I'll be mine
And we'll tak' a cup o' kindness yet,
For auld lang syne.

III
We twa hae run about the braes
And pu'd he gowans fine;

But we've wandered mony a weary foot,
Sin auld lang syne.

IV

We twa hae paidl'd i' the burn
Frae mornin' sun till dine;
But seas between us braid hae roar'd
Sin auld lang syne.

V

And there's a hand, my trusty fiere!
And gie's a hand o' thine!
And we'll tak' a right guid-willy waught,
For auld lang syne.

It is the chorus that people get wrong in particular, and yet it is the one part of the song they think they know perfectly well. The anglicized version of the chorus is:

For auld lang syne, my dear,
For auld lang syne,
We'll take a cup of kindness yet,
For auld lang syne.

The problem arises not in the replacement of "my jo" for "my dear" but because most people sing the last line as "For the sake of auld lang syne." It is not clear how the words "the sake of" have snuck into the lyrics, but it would appear that they are well and truly stuck there now in the public consciousness.

Did ye ken . . . ?

In most large department stores in Japan, "Auld Lang Syne" is played on a daily basis to mark closing time.

WHO INVENTED THE
MACINTOSH?

ontrary to popular belief, and as you will have discovered for yourself by now (if you've read this book from cover to cover) the Scots invented none of the following—bagpipes, kilts, porridge, whisky, or tartan. They didn't even invent Scotland itself for that matter! However, Scots did invent or discover all of the following, many of which it would be hard to imagine our world without today:

Adhesive postage stamps
Bicycle pedals
The breech-loading rifle
Car insurance
Chloroform
Color photography
The cure for malaria

The Bank of England
Bovril
Carbon dioxide
The cell nucleus
The cloud chamber
Corn flour
The decimal point

Great Scot!

James Watt (1736–1819) invented the first efficient steam engine at a time when the new factories of the Industrial Revolution needed power desperately. He began making his engines with Matthew Boulton, and new improvements were made with every new engine. The machines used air pressure as well as steam to make the piston work more effectively. "Sun and planet" gears turned the wheels or rotated a shaft to drive factory machinery. Watt coined the term "horsepower" to describe how powerful his rotative engines were, and he even gave his name to the unit of electrical power, the "Watt," such was his impact on the world of science and engineering.

Electromagnetism
The *Encyclopaedia Britannica*
The fax machine
Fingerprinting
The fountain pen
Hypnosis
Hypodermic syringes

Insulin
The kaleidoscope
The Kelvin scale
Latent heat
The lawn mower
Lime cordial
Logarithms

Marmalade
The MRI scanner
The paddle steamer
Paraffin
Penicillin
Piano pedals

Pneumatic tires
Polarization
The postmark
Radar
The raincoat
The reaping machine

Great Scot!

Alexander Fleming (1881–1955) accidentally left the lid off a small round dish of germs he was studying in 1928. He noticed that the germs on the dish were dying and, when he investigated further, Fleming discovered that some microscopic spores of fungus, or mold, had floated into the dish, and it was these that were killing the bacteria. Fleming identified the mold as *Penicillium*, and he called the germ-killing chemical it made "penicillin." Fleming's work was taken up by Australian medical scientist Howard Florey and German chemist Ernst Chain. It was they who discovered how to make large amounts of penicillin, which became the first antibiotic or bacteria-killing drug. Penicillin was used during World War II to treat the infected wounds of soldiers and since then it and other antibiotics have saved millions of lives.

The reflecting telescope
The refrigerator
Savings banks
The screw propeller
The speedometer
The steam engine

The teleprinter
Television
Trucks
Tubular steel
The typhoid vaccine
The ultrasound scanner

Great Scot!

Charles Macintosh (1766–1834) was a Scottish chemist who invented the weatherproof fabric that was the basis of the raincoat that now bears his name. The name Macintosh is now used to describe any waterproof coat, but it originally described a raincoat made of the rubberized cloth that he had patented. In 1819 Macintosh discovered that India rubber would dissolve in naphtha (a coal-tar product), and that this solution could be painted onto pieces of woollen cloth. Pressed together, they produced a waterproof fabric that could be tailored into a garment. In 1830, Macintosh and his partner Thomas Hancock began to manufacture ready-to-wear raincoats in Glasgow, but these new Macintoshes were criticized for being smelly and looking like sacks!

The steam hammer
Tarmac
The telephone
Universal Standard Time

Vacuum flasks
Wave-Powered electricity generators
Wire rope

Did ye ken . . . ?

Uncle Sam, the national personification of the United States, was based on New York businessman Samuel Wilson, whose parents had sailed to America from Greenock on the Clyde in Scotland. During the War of 1812, he provided the army with beef and pork in barrels that were labeled "U.S." for United States. However, the joke soon got around that the letters stood for "Uncle Sam," and soon the term was being used to refer to the federal government.

Great Scot!

James Watt (1736–1819) invented the first efficient steam engine at a time when the new factories of the Industrial Revolution needed power desperately. He began making his engines with Matthew Boulton, and new improvements were made with every new engine. The machines used air pressure as well as steam to make the piston work more effectively. "Sun and planet" gears turned the wheels or rotated a shaft to drive factory machinery. Watt coined the term "horsepower" to describe how powerful his rotative engines were, and he even gave his name to the unit of electrical power, the "Watt," such was his impact on the world of science and engineering.

Scotland isn't just known for its scientific thinkers and inventors either; there is also a thriving literary tradition, and a number of books that are today considered classics were written by Scottish authors.

Ten Scottish Literary Legends

1. J. M. Barrie—*Peter Pan*
2. Robert Louis Stevenson—*Treasure Island, The Strange Case of Dr. Jekyll and Mr. Hyde*
3. Sir Arthur Conan Doyle—*The Adventures of Sherlock Holmes, The Lost World*
4. Iain [M.] Banks—*Consider Phlebas, The Crow Road*
5. Val McDermid—the mistress of Tartan noir, author of the *Wire in the Blood* books featuring psychologist Dr. Tony Hill
6. Ian Rankin—the Inspector Rebus novels
7. Nigel Tranter—many historical Scottish novels, including *MacBeth the King*
8. Irvine Welsh—*Trainspotting*
9. Kenneth Grahame—*The Wind in the Willows*
10. Alexander McCall Smith—The No. 1 Ladies' Detective Agency

Some of the most enduring and popular comics in the United Kingdom are Scottish creations. The famous and long-lasting *Oor Wullie* and *The Broons* are both products of publisher D. C. Thompson, as are *The Beano* and *The Dandy*. Even seminal British sci-fi, fantasy, and horror comic *2000AD* was originally created for D. C. Thompson, and two of its most well-known writers, John Wagner (*A History of Violence*) and Alan Grant (*Batman*), both hail from Scotland.

Scottish Americans have had no less an impact on the world either. Technically, a Scots American is a citizen of the United States whose ancestry originates, either wholly or partly, in Scotland. 2008's American Community Survey discovered that Scottish Americans made up an estimated 1.9 percent of the total population of the United States, and the number of Americans of Scottish descent now outnumber the population of Scotland.

Did ye ken . . . ?

Although born in England, author and creator of the Harry Potter novels, J. K. Rowling (a.k.a. Joanne Murray) has been adopted by the Scots as one of their writers. This is in part because in 2001 she married Neil Michael Murray, an anesthetist, lives in Scotland at Killiechassie House on the banks of the River Tay, and is even a member of the Church of Scotland. She also has honorary degrees from the University of St Andrews, the University of Edinburgh, Napier University, and the University of Aberdeen. She also has the honor of being the first billionaire author.

Famous Americans who trace their family tree back to its roots in Scotland include film stars, presidents, and multibillionaires. Here are just a few of them, both past and present.

Ben Affleck—actor
Jennifer Aniston—actress
Billie Joe Armstrong—singer and guitarist with the band Green Day
Lance Armstrong—seven-time winner of the Tour de France
Lucille Ball—actress
Kristen Bell—actress
Linda Blair—actor most famous for her role in 1973's seminal horror film *The Exorcist*
Jack Black—actor, singer, and comedian
Jim Bowie—frontiersman and a defender of the Alamo
David Dunbar Buick—founder of the Buick Motor Company
William Wallace Campbell—astronomer

Drew Carey—comedy actor and game show host

Andrew Carnegie—industrialist and philanthropist who donated millions of dollars to libraries and arts and education institutions in the United States and Great Britain

Johnny Cash—singer

Alice Cooper—rock star

James Fenimore Cooper—author, best known for writing *The Last of the Mohicans*

Samuel W. Crawford—U.S. Army surgeon and Union general in the American Civil War

Michael Crichton—author, most famous for *Jurassic Park*

Davy Crockett—frontiersman, U.S. Congressman, and one of the defenders of the Alamo

Miley Cyrus—actor and singer, also known as Hannah Montana

Matt Damon—actor

Jasper Newton "Jack" Daniel—founder of Jack Daniel's Tennessee whiskey distillery

James Dean—actor

Donald Wills Douglas, Sr—launched the world's first commercial passenger plane, the DC-3, in 1935

Robert Downey, Jr—actor, most recently seen playing the roles of Iron Man and Sherlock Holmes, the creation of Scottish writer Sir Arthur Conan Doyle

David Duchovny—actor

Clint Eastwood—actor and director

William Faulkner—won the Nobel Prize for Literature in 1949

Stacy "Fergie" Ferguson—singer with The Black Eyed Peas

Brandon Flowers—singer and keyboardist of The Killers

B. C. Forbes—journalist and founder of *Forbes* Magazine

Alexander Garden—botanist, physician, and zoologist who gave his name to the gardenia

Bill Gates—cofounder of the software giant Microsoft and, until only recently, the richest man in the world, being a billionaire more than fifty times over

Mel Gibson—actor and director, most notably of *Braveheart*, of the Clan Buchanan

Jay Gould—railroad developer

Larry Hagman—actor, best known for J. R. Ewing on *Dallas*

Oscar Hammerstein II—writer of musicals

Oliver Hardy—comedy actor

Jennifer Love Hewitt—actress, producer, and singer

Tommy Hilfiger—fashion designer

" No people so few in number have scored
so deep a mark in the world's history as the
Scots have done. No people
have a greater right to be proud of their blood. "

—JAMES ANTHONY FROUDE